KENTUCKY

ENVIRONMENTAL LAW HANDBOOK

Third Edition

Prepared by
Greenebaum Doll & McDonald PLLC

Senior Editor
Lloyd R. Cress

Associate Editor
Kelly A. Dant

Contributing Editors
Carolyn M. Brown
Martin J. Cunningham III
Bradley E. Dillon
Marcus P. McGraw

Government Institutes
A Division of ABS Group Inc.
Rockville, Maryland

Government Institutes, a Division of ABS Group Inc.
4 Research Place, Rockville, Maryland 20850, USA
Phone: (301) 921-2300
Fax: (301) 921-0373
Email: giinfo@govinst.com
Internet: http://www.govinst.com

Published April 2001.

05 04 03 02 01 5 4 3 2 1

ISBN: 978-0-86587-831-0

Printed in the United States of America

TABLE OF CONTENTS

PREFACE

This edition of the Kentucky Environmental Law Handbook is intended to provide a general overview of the environmental law requirements applicable in the Commonwealth of Kentucky. The publication is intended to assist persons seeking a general familiarity with such requirements and to identify specific aspects of their implementation in Kentucky that may differ from their implementation at the federal level and in other states.

In this edition each program area is addressed initially by reference to the federal statutes or regulations that provide the backdrop for the development of Kentucky-specific program requirements. These are followed by references to and/or discussion of the Kentucky programs that implement the federal programs.

This edition is not intended to serve as legal advice regarding specific environmental law issues. Advice regarding such issues must take into account a myriad of factors that are beyond the scope of this publication.

ABOUT THE FIRM

Greenbaum Doll & McDonald PLLC is a full-service law firm of over 170 attorneys with offices in Louisville, Lexington, Covington, and Frankfort, Kentucky and in Cincinnati, Ohio and Nashville, Tennessee. The firm has been engaged in the practice of law for almost 50 years and is routinely recognized for its devotion to client service. The Firm's mission is to provide clients value-adding services and solutions that enable them to achieve their business and personal objectives.

GD&M was one of the first regional law firms to recognize the value of its attorneys concentrating their practices in specific areas of law. The Firm has instituted a practice group management structure to serve client needs, including an Environmental and Natural Resources Practice Group.

Greenebaum Doll & McDonald PLLC offers a full range of environmental law services to clients. Its attorneys have extensive experience in counseling clients regarding compliance with environmental requirements including the Clean Air Act, Clean Water Act, Resource Conservation and Recovery Act, Comprehensive Environmental Response, Compensation and Liability Act and comparable state and local regulatory programs.

GREENEBAUM DOLL & MCDONALD PLLC

3300 National City Tower
101 South Fifth Street
Louisville, Kentucky 40202
(502) 589-4200

333 West Vine Street
Suite 1400
Lexington, Kentucky 40507
(859) 231-8500

Suite 1800
50 East River Center Blvd.
Covington, Kentucky 41011
(859) 655-4200

229 West Main Street
Suite 100
Frankfort, Kentucky 40601-1847
(502) 875-0050

700 Two American Center
3102 West End Ave.
Nashville, Tennessee 37203
(615) 760-7100

2800 Chemed Center
255 East Fifth Street
Cincinnati, Ohio 45202
(513) 455-7600

ABOUT THE AUTHORS

This edition of the Kentucky Environmental Law Handbook is the collective effort of the Environmental and Natural Resources Practice Group of Greenebaum Doll & McDonald PLLC.

SENIOR EDITOR

Lloyd R. Cress is counsel to the firm in its Lexington office and previously served as Chairman of its Environmental and Natural Resources Practice Group. He has practiced exclusively in the area of environmental law for the past 34 years.

Mr. Cress graduated from the University of Kentucky in 1960 and from the University of Kentucky College of Law in 1962. He served as Assistant Attorney General for the Commonwealth of Kentucky's environmental agencies from 1967 to 1969 and as chief environmental counsel for Ashland Inc. from 1969 until entering the private practice of law in 1981. He is a past vice-chairman of the Water Quality Section of the American Bar Association and a past chairman of the American Petroleum Institute Environmental Law Committee.

Mr. Cress currently serves as environmental law advisor to the Kentucky Chamber of Commerce.

ASSOCIATE EDITOR

Kelly A. Dant, an associate of the firm, concentrates in environmental law and general litigation. She is resident in the Lexington office.

Ms. Dant received her Bachelor of Science in Biology from Morehead State University and her Juris Doctor from the University of Kentucky College of Law. While at the University of Kentucky she served on the staff of the Journal of Natural Resources and Environmental Law and as Vice President of the Environmental Law Society. She is a member of the Kentucky and Fayette County Bar Associations and has also been admitted before the Eastern and Western Districts of Kentucky.

CONTRIBUTING EDITORS

Carolyn M. Brown, a member of the firm and chair of the firm's Environmental and Natural Resources Practice Group, concentrates in environmental law and litigation, particularly in matters relating to air, water and hazardous waste compliance as well as permitting. She is resident in the Lexington office.

Ms. Brown received her Bachelor of Science from the University of Kentucky and her Juris Doctor from the University of Kentucky College of Law. While at the University of Kentucky, she served on the Moot Court Board and the staff of the Kentucky Law Journal. Among other honors, she was awarded the Order of the Coif.

Ms. Brown is a member of the Kentucky and the Texas bar and has also been admitted before the U.S. Court of Appeals, Fifth, Sixth and D.C. Circuits as well as the U.S. District Courts for the Eastern and Western Districts of Kentucky and the Northern District of Texas.

She is a member of the American and Kentucky Bar Associations. She currently serves as Vice-Chair of the Local Emergency Planning Committee for Fayette County and is a past chair of the Natural Resources Law Section of the Kentucky Bar Association.

Martin J. Cunningham III, counsel to the firm in its Lexington office, has concentrated in environmental law for the past twenty years.

Mr. Cunningham received his Bachelor of Science from Eastern Kentucky University and his Juris Doctor from Chase College of Law. He served as a Kentucky Special Assistant Attorney General for environmental matters while employed with the Kentucky Natural Resources and Environmental Protection Cabinet from 1980 until 1987.

He is a member of the Kentucky bar and is admitted to practice before the U.S. District Court, Western District of Kentucky and the U.S. District Court, Eastern District of Kentucky.

Bradley E. Dillon is a member of the law firm of Greenebaum Doll & McDonald PLLC. Mr. Dillon has practiced in the environmental field for over 20 years and has worked for a regulatory agency, as in-house counsel for a publicly traded company that managed both hazardous and nuclear wastes, as well as in private practice. Mr. Dillon most frequently represents companies in Clean Air Act and hazardous waste permitting and enforcement issues, as well as in transactional negotiations where environmental conditions become significant issues. He is a certified Risk Manager and has extensive experience in assessing the role of environmental insurance as a tool to protect buyers and sellers of contaminated properties.

Marcus P. McGraw is a member of the firm, concentrates in environmental law, administrative law and mineral law. He is resident in the Lexington office.

Mr. McGraw received his Bachelor of Arts from the University of North Carolina, Chapel Hill and his Juris Doctor from George Washington University Law School. He has served as a trial attorney for the Office of the Solicitor, Mine Safety & Health Division and Assistant Solicitor for Litigation and Enforcement, Division of Surface Mining, U.S. Department of the Interior, Washington, D.C.

He is a member of the Kentucky and Maryland bar and has also been admitted before the District of Columbia, U.S. District Courts for the Eastern District of Kentucky and the District of Columbia and the U.S. Court of Appeals, Sixth Circuit.

He is a member of Kentucky Bar Association Natural Resources Section, the Kentucky Crushed Stone Association - Health & Safety Committee, the Kentucky Coal Association - Safety & Environmental Committee and the Kentucky Ready-Mixed Concrete Association. He co-authors a quarterly newsletter called Mine Safety and Health Bulletin. Mr. McGraw has authored numerous articles on environmental, mineral and administrative law issues and is a frequent speaker on these topics.

OVERVIEW

Environmental programs in Kentucky generally consist of federal environmental laws that are administered by state agencies under the federalism concept. Kentucky has been delegated authority to administer key programs under the Clean Water Act, the Clean Air Act, some portions of the Safe Drinking Water Act (not including the Underground Injection Control Program), the Resource Conservation and Recovery Act and the Surface Mining Control and Reclamation Act. The Kentucky Natural Resources and Environmental Protection Cabinet is the state agency having primary responsibility for carrying out the federally-delegated environmental control programs. A summary of the environmental permit programs administered by the Cabinet is provided in Appendix A of this publication.

Certain federal environmental programs such as the National Environmental Policy Act and the Comprehensive Environmental Response Compensation and Liability Act do not contain provisions authorizing delegation to state authorities. Accordingly, those programs are administered by the United States Environmental Protection Agency (USEPA) Region IV offices in Atlanta, Georgia. USEPA Region IV also exercises federal oversight of most of the federal environmental programs for which primary responsibility has been delegated to Kentucky.

CHAPTER 1

Legal Framework for Environmental Law in Kentucky

Kentucky's Constitution contains no provisions relating to environmental protection. Accordingly, the basic environmental law of Kentucky is set forth in the Kentucky Revised Statutes (KRS) and the Kentucky Administrative Regulations (KAR). Additionally, a few environmental regulatory programs are based upon municipal or other local government ordinances enacted pursuant to authority conferred by state statutes.

KRS Chapter 224 is the primary statutory authority under which Kentucky's environmental programs are conducted. The statute was initially enacted in 1972 and has been subsequently amended on numerous occasions. KRS Chapter 224 includes the following subchapters:

- Subchapter 1 - General; Environmental Quality Commission; Environmental Trust Fund; Environmental Emergencies.

- Subchapter 10 - Natural Resources and Environmental Protection Cabinet; Organization; Powers and Functions; Operational Procedures; Hearing Procedures; Programs

- Subchapter 16 - State-Federal Relations

- Subchapter 18 - Interstate Relations; Interstate Environmental Compact; Interstate Compact on Air Pollution; Interstate Water Sanitation; Interstate Compact on Solid Waste Management

- Subchapter 20 - Air Quality; Air Pollution Control; Asbestos Control; Small Business Stationary Sources; Vehicle Emission Control

- Subchapter 30 - Noise Control

- Subchapter 40 - Waste; General Provisions; Waste Permits and Licensing; Operating Requirements

- Subchapter 43 - Solid Waste; General Provisions; Planning and Management; Limited Quantity Hazardous Waste; Assistance Programs; Demonstration Projects

- Chapter 46 - Hazardous Waste; Center for Hazardous Waste Reduction; Planning and Management

- Subchapter 50 - Specific Types of Waste - Agricultural Chemicals; Chemical Munitions; Lead Acid Batteries; Used Oil; Plastic Containers; Special Wastes; Tires

- Subchapter 60 - Underground Storage Facilities

- Subchapter 70 - Water Quality

- Subchapter 71 - Agriculture Water Quality

- Subchapter 73 - Sewage Treatment

- Subchapter 99 - Penalties

In addition to KRS Chapter 224, several other KRS Chapters establish environmental programs applicable to specific subject matters. These include the following:

- KRS Chapter 77 - Local pollution control districts

- KRS Chapter 100 - Planning and zoning

- KRS Chapter 109 - Local solid waste management

- KRS Chapter 149 - Forestry

- KRS Chapter 150 - Fish and wildlife resources

- KRS Chapter 151 - Geology and water resources

- KRS Chapter 211 - State health programs

- KRS Chapter 212 - Local health programs

- KRS Chapter 220 - Sanitation districts

- KRS Chapter 224A - Kentucky Infrastructure Authority

- KRS Chapter 350-353 - Mines and Minerals
- KRS Chapter 262 - Soil and Water Conservation

CHAPTER 2

Organizational Structure of Natural Resources and Environmental Protection Cabinet

The Kentucky Natural Resources and Environmental Protection (NREPC) is the administrative agency having primary responsibility for environmental programs in Kentucky. NREPC was created under legislation enacted in 1972 which abolished the Kentucky Water Pollution Control Commission and the Kentucky Air Pollution Control Commission and transferred environmental protection functions from the Kentucky Department of Health to the newly-created NREPC.

The principal executive authority of the NREPC is vested in the Office of the Secretary. The Secretary has ultimate responsibility for the promulgation of administrative regulations and the determination of contested cases such as enforcement actions and permit appeals. The Office of the Secretary also supervises generally the operation of the departments that comprise NREPC. The most recent organizational charts for NREPC, its Department for Environmental Protection and certain divisions within the Department for Environmental Protection are provided in Appendix B to this publication.

The Office of the Secretary conducts its administrative functions through the Office of Administrative Hearings, the Office of Legal Services, the Office of Information Services, the Office of Inspector General and the Division of Administrative Services. Although each of these agencies has a significant role in the day-to-day function of the Cabinet, the Office of Legal Services and the Office of Administrative Hearings perform functions that impact directly on persons subject to regulation by NREPC.

The Office of Legal Services provides legal services to each of the departments through which NREPC conducts it regulatory activities. The director of the Office of Legal Services serves as the general counsel for NREPC and is the principal legal advisor to the Secretary. The Office of

Legal Services functions independently of the state Attorney General's office although their functions and duties may overlap in certain very limited instances.

The Office of Administrative Hearings has responsibility for conducting administrative contested case hearings before NREPC. The Office of Administrative Hearings' staff includes a number of attorneys who serve as hearing officers on administrative cases.

NREPC conducts its regulatory activities through three departments - the Department for Environmental Protection, the Department for Natural Resources and the Department for Surface Mining Reclamation and Enforcement. Each department is headed by a commissioner and is subdivided into divisions which are headed by directors.

The Department for Environmental Protection has authority for implementation of media-specific environmental regulatory programs. Accordingly, the Department for Environmental Protection is organized into the Division for Air Quality, the Division of Water, and the Division of Waste Management. The Department for Environmental Protection also includes a Division of Environmental Services which provides technical support such as laboratory analytical services to the other divisions within the Department.

The Division for Air Quality is organized into the following branches:

- Program Planning and Administration Branch
- Permit Review Branch
- Technical Services Branch

- Field Operations Branch
- Special Programs Branch, and
- Enforcement Branch.

The Division of Water consists of the following branches:

- Water Quality Branch
- Drinking Water Branch
- Water Resources Branch
- Program Planning and Administration Branch
- Kentucky Pollutant Discharge Elimination System (KPDES) Branch
- Groundwater Branch
- Facilities Construction Branch, and
- Enforcement Branch.

The Division of Waste Management is subdivided into the following branches:

- Program Planning and Administration Branch
- Solid Waste Branch
- Hazardous Waste Branch
- Superfund Branch
- Field Operations Branch
- Enforcement Branch
- Underground Storage Tank Branch, and
- Resource Conservation and Local Assistance Branch.

Each branch is headed by a branch manager.

The Department for Environmental Protection's principal office is in Frankfort, Kentucky. It has field offices located in Ashland, Bowling Green, Columbia, Florence, Frankfort, Hazard, London, Louisville, Madisonville, Morehead, Owensboro, and Paducah. Not all of the field offices conduct regulatory activities for all of the environmental media within the jurisdiction of the Department for Environmental Protection.

The Department for Natural Resources has responsibility for regulatory activities involving natural resources other than minerals. The Department for Natural Resources is organized into the Division of Forestry, the Division of Conservation and the Division of Energy.

The Department of Surface Mining Reclamation and Enforcement has primary responsibility for the regulation of coal mining and other non-coal mineral extraction. The Department of Surface Mining Reclamation and Enforcement is comprised of the Division of Permits, the Division of Field Services and the Division of Abandoned Mine Lands.

The Environmental Quality Commission (EQC) is a body created pursuant to KRS 224.01-100 through KRS 224.01-115. EQC is attached to NREPC for administrative purposes. The principal role of EQC is to advise the Governor and the Secretary of NREPC on environmental matters. Additionally, EQC serves as a public forum for discussion of environmental issues. EQC also has a limited role in NREPC's administrative rule-making process which will be addressed in more detail in Section X.

EQC consists of seven (7) members appointed by the Governor for staggered terms. A majority of the Commission's membership must be persons who do not hold a permit issued by the Cabinet or represent entities that hold such a permit.

CHAPTER 3

Water Quality

A. NPDES/KPDES Permit Program

The most significant program regulating water quality in Kentucky is the National Pollutant Discharge Elimination System (NPDES) permit program established by Section 402 of the Clean Water Act.[1] The NPDES permit program prohibits the discharge of pollutants into waters of the United States except where authorized by permit. USEPA has delegated NPDES permit program authority to NREPC where it is administered as the Kentucky Pollutant Discharge Elimination System (KPDES) permit program. USEPA retains oversight of the KPDES permit program and has the right to veto permits that are inconsistent with the Clean Water Act.

The state-implemented KPDES permit program is virtually a picture image of the federal NPDES permit program by virtue of KRS 224.16-050 which prohibits NREPC from issuing KPDES permits with effluent limitations, monitoring requirements or other conditions more stringent than would have been included in a NPDES permit.

Since the NPDES permit program requires that a permit be held for the"discharge of a pollutant"[2] to "waters of the United States"[3], the meaning of those terms is a critical factor in

---

1 33 U.S.C. Section 1342

2 33 U.S.C. Section 1362(12)

3 33 U.S.C. Section 1362(7)

determining the scope of the program. The courts have construed those terms very broadly. As a result, most discharges that reach waterways are subject to the KPDES permit program.

One significant limitation on the scope of the KPDES permit program is that it applies only to "point source"[4] discharges. A point source is any "discernible, confined, and discrete conveyance"[5] through which pollutants may be discharged and includes pipes, ditches and other conduits. The courts have tended to consider virtually any discharge other than uncontrolled sheet runoff of storm water to be a point source discharge. For example, courts have construed the term to include storm water runoff that is channeled by curbs or gutters or that is directed by berms or surface contours that have been changed to control or redirect the flow.[6] Additionally, the courts have held that wastewater discharges are point source discharges subject to the NPDES permit program if, at any time, they have been under human control even though their ultimate discharge may not take place through a pipe.[7]

The applicability of the NPDES/KPDES permit program has also been expanded by the courts by broad interpretations of the term "pollutants". That term has been construed to include not only the physical and chemical constituents that have been commonly considered to cause pollution but also such conditions as heat and flow.[8]

---

4 33 U.S.C. Section 1362(14)

5 33 U.S.C. Section 1362(14)

6 U.S. v. Earth Sciences, 599 F.2d 368 (10th Cir. 1979)

7 Sierra Club v. Abston Construction Company 620 F.2d 41 (5th Cir. 1980)

8 33 U.S.C. Section 1362(6)

The jurisdictional term "waters of the United States" has similarly been broadly construed by the courts to encompass virtually all waterways that receive discharges of wastewater either directly or indirectly. The courts have held that Congress, in using that term, intended it to apply to all waters that Congress has the power to regulate under its authority over interstate commerce.[9]

The NPDES/KPDES permit program does not apply to several categories of discharges. For example, discharges to publicly owned treatment works are regulated through permits issued to the public agency rather than to the source of the wastewater. The source of the wastewater is considered to be an indirect discharger subject to regulation under pretreatment standards and under local wastewater control programs and is not subject to the NPDES/KPDES permit program.[10]

Other types of wastewater discharges that are not subject to the NPDES/KPDES permit program include the land application of pollutants without runoff to waters of the United States, some discharges from watercraft, discharges of dredge and fill material that are subject to regulation under Section 404 of the Clean Water Act, discharges to groundwater that has no direct nexus with surface water and, some discharges of storm water.[11]

One of the most controversial KPDES permit issues in Kentucky involves the applicability of the permit requirement to discharges to groundwater particularly in areas of karst terrain. Although Section 402 of the Clean Water Act limits the permit requirement to

---

9 U.S. v. Ashland Oil and Transportation 504 F.2d 1317 (6th Cir. 1974)

10 401 KAR 5:055 Section 1(2)(c)

11 401 KAR 5:055 Section 1(2)

discharges to "waters of the United States" thereby including surface waters but excluding ground waters, the KPDES permit program regulation 401 KAR 5:055 extends the requirement to discharges to "waters of the Commonwealth" which is defined in KRS 224.01-010 to include groundwaters. The apparent regulatory extension of the KPDES permit program to discharges to ground water is negated, however, by KRS 224.16-050 which prohibits Kentucky's KPDES permit program from being more stringent than the federal NPDES permit program.

Another controversial aspect of this issue involves the physical characteristics of karst terrain. Since groundwater in karst terrain can flow in well-defined channels before it reaches the surface, discharges to such waters could arguably be said to be discharges to surface water if the groundwater has a clear nexus with surface water. Nevertheless NREPC has held that the land application of wastewater in areas of karst terrain that finds its way by virtue of the hydrologic cycle into subsurface channels where it eventually reaches surface water is not subject to the KPDES permit program.[12]

KPDES permit program regulation 401 KAR 5:060 establishes the procedures for the issuance of KPDES permits. Under the regulation, applications for new KPDES permits must be submitted no later than 180 days prior to the commencement of the discharge. Similarly, applications for the renewal of currently-effective KPDES permits must be submitted no later than 180 days prior to the expiration of the current permit. If a complete application for renewal of an existing KPDES permit is submitted in a timely manner and final action is not taken on the application until after the expiration date of the expiring permit, the expiring permit will continue in effect until final action is taken on the application for renewal.

---

[12] Sierra Club v. NREPC; Cagles-Keystone (DOW23778-043; 1998)

Upon receipt of a complete KPDES permit application, the NREPC Division of Water will issue a draft permit containing terms and conditions such as effluent limitations, monitoring requirements, reporting requirements and compliance schedules if appropriate. A fact sheet or statement of basis will also be issued by the Division of Water which will describe the discharge to be authorized under the permit and the technical and legal issues addressed in the permit.

The draft KPDES permit will be submitted to public notice and comment for a period of 30 days after its issuance. Although the KPDES permit program regulations provide for public hearings where there is a significant degree of public interest in a draft permit[13], the Division of Water procedure has been to conduct such a hearing whenever there is a request for a public hearing. KPDES permit regulation 401 KAR 5:075 provides that issues must be raised during the public comment period if they are to be considered in adjudication of the final permit action. The final KPDES permit action will include a response to issues raised during the public comment period. Final administrative action on KPDES permit applications takes effect 30 days after issuance except in certain limited instances.

KPDES permits are issued for a term not to exceed five years. Although the Division of Water has historically issued virtually all permits with the maximum five year duration, the Division is currently writing permits with expiration dates that coincide with the expiration dates of all other KPDES permits in the watershed receiving the discharge. By having all KPDES permits in a watershed expire simultaneously, the Division expects to be in a position to implement watershed basin planning more effectively.

---

[13] 401 KAR 5:075 Section 7

KPDES permits specify effluent limitations and monitoring and reporting requirements. KPDES permits also incorporate by reference the general conditions applicable to all KPDES permits that appear in 401 KAR 5:065.

Effluent limitations in KPDES permits may be either technology-based or water quality-based. Under the Clean Water Act all such permits must, at a minimum, require compliance with applicable technology-based standards.[14] Additionally, the permits must require compliance with water quality-based limitations if compliance with technology-based limitations would not achieve compliance with in-stream water quality standards.[15]

The technology-based limitations of KPDES permits are derived from Section 301 of the Clean Water Act[16] which requires industrial and other non-public discharges to apply best practicable control technology (BPT); best available technology economically achievable (BAT) for toxic and non-conventional pollutants; and best conventional pollutant control technology (BCT) for conventional pollutants such as solids and organic matter. Publicly-owned treatment works (POTW) must apply secondary treatment and best practicable waste treatment technology.

USEPA has established by federal regulation nationally applicable technology-based effluent guidelines limitations for various categories of discharges. The categorical effluent limitations generally limit the mass of pollutants that can be discharged (pounds or kilograms) on a per unit of production basis. For certain categories of discharges the technology-based effluent

---

[14] 33 U.S.C. 1311

[15] 33 U.S.C. 1311(b)(1)(c)

[16] 33 U.S.C. 1311

limitations are expressed in terms of concentration (milligrams per liter) of pollutants in the wastewater discharge. Limitations are generally stated as monthly average and daily maximum amounts. Federal categorical effluent limitations are incorporated by reference in 401 KAR 5:065 and are included as KPDES permit conditions without consideration of their necessity to achieve in-stream water quality objectives.

Discharges that are in industrial categories for which no effluent guidelines have been promulgated on a national basis are issued KPDES permits with effluent limitations reflecting the best professional judgment (BPJ) of the permit writer as to the effluent quality that would be achieved by application of the level of technology required by Section 301 of the Clean Water Act. KPDES permit conditions reflecting BPJ determinations are inherently subjective and, unlike effluent limitations based upon categorical standards, are subject to negotiation and/or litigation as to the BPJ determination.

401 KAR 5:065(7) provides for the adjustment of KPDES permit effluent limitations to account for pollutants that are present in the discharger's intake water. Such an adjustment is referred to as a net-gross credit and is available only to meet technology-based limitations when requested by the permittee during the permit application process.

If compliance with technology-based effluent limitations will not achieve compliance with in-stream water quality standards, the KPDES permit must include water quality-based effluent limitations. Water quality-based effluent limitations may be developed to comply with instream numeric standards for specific substances or to comply with narrative standards such as a prohibition against in-stream toxicity. When the water quality-based effluent limitations are developed to comply with a chemical-specific standard, the limitations are calculated through a waste load allocation process using simulation modeling of stream flow conditions, in-stream background levels of pollutants, and the manner in which the discharged pollutants mix with the receiving stream. When the water quality-based effluent limitation is developed to comply with a narrative standard, such as a prohibition against in-stream toxicity, the limitation may take the form of a whole effluent toxicity limitation enforced through biomonitoring provisions.

The Division of Water's practices in the issuance of KPDES permits containing water quality-based effluent limitations include the following:

- Effluent limitations for discharges to streams with no flow at critical low-flow periods are established at the water quality standard protective against chronic effects;
- Effluent limitations for discharges to streams with flow but without a submerged diffuser are established at the water quality standard protective against acute effects unless more stringent limitations are necessary to protect against chronic effects;
- Critical low-flow conditions ($7Q_{10}$) are used in performing waste load allocations unless the discharger can control the wastewater and release it during periods of greater flow.

The issuance of KPDES permits containing water quality-based effluent limitations involves numerous factual assumptions. Accordingly, such permits lend themselves to negotiation and litigation.

The effluent limitations in KPDES permits are enforced through self-monitoring and reporting under permit conditions that specify the type of sampling to be conducted and the frequency of sampling and reporting. Permittees submit Discharge Monitoring Reports (DMR) to the Division of Water providing information regarding the monitoring and analysis of the effluent.

Under the KPDES permit program regulations, KPDES permits may contain schedules of compliance consistent with Clean Water Act deadlines. However, the statutory deadline for compliance with technology-based effluent limitations has passed and schedules of compliance are no longer available to meet such requirements. Schedules of compliance remain available, however, where necessary to meet newly-imposed water quality-based effluent limitations such as new whole effluent toxicity limitations.

401 KAR 5:065 prohibits KPDES permittees from bypassing any portion of their wastewater treatment system except under very limited circumstances. For example, a bypass that does not result in a violation of effluent limitations may be authorized if its is for essential maintenance to assure efficient operation. Other bypasses are subject to enforcement unless it is necessary to prevent loss of life, personal injury or severe property damage.

The KPDES permit program is, with very limited exceptions, an absolute liability program in that exceedances of permit limitations constitute violations notwithstanding the level of care exercised by the permittee. One of the very few exceptions to absolute liability involves non-complying discharges resulting from upset conditions. 401 KAR 5:065 Section 1 (14) provides that it is an affirmative defense to alleged non-compliance with a technology-based effluent limitation if the permittee can establish that an upset occurred and the permittee can identify the cause of the upset, that the permitted facility was being properly operated, that the permittee gave timely notice to the Division of Water of the occurrence of the upset, and that the permittee took necessary remedial action.

USEPA regulations implementing the NPDES permit program authorize the issuance of general permits in lieu of individual permits under certain circumstances.[17] NREPC Division of Water regulation 401 KAR 5:055 provides for the issuance of KPDES general permits for storm

---

[17] 40 CFR 122.28

water discharges for categories of discharges that have similar operations, discharge similar wastewater and involve similar effluent limitations and monitoring requirements. General KPDES permits are not issued for specific sources but are instead issued for a category of sources. Dischargers who seek authorization to discharge under a general KPDES permit are not required to submit a KPDES permit application but instead submit a notice of intent to be covered by the general KPDES permit. The Division of Water does not charge a fee to persons who seek coverage under a general KPDES permit because there is no permit application to be processed by the Division. Dischargers that have been issued an individual KPDES permit are not eligible for coverage under a general permit. Dischargers may, at their option, apply for individual KPDES permits rather than be covered by a general KPDES permit.

General KPDES permits have been issued by the Division of Water for several categories of discharges. A general KPDES permit has been issued for discharges from coal mining activities and most coal mining operations are covered by the general permit. General KPDES permits have also been issued for storm water discharges from several categories of activities and most storm water discharges are regulated under general rather than individual KPDES permits.

The Clean Water Act provides for the regulation of point source discharges of storm water from certain types of activities. Storm water discharges that are associated with industrial activity and storm water discharges from large and medium-sized municipal storm water systems are presently regulated. The NREPC Division of Water has incorporated USEPA's storm water regulations into administrative regulation 401 KAR 5:060.

The Division of Water regulation provides for regulation under the KPDES permit program of storm water from the following categories of activities associated with industrial activity:

- Facilities subject to storm water effluent limitations guidelines, new source performance standards, or toxic pollutant standards;

- Most facilities within SIC codes 24, 26, 28, 29, 311, 32, 33, 3441 and 373 which relate to certain manufacturing activities;

- Most facilities within SIC codes 10 through 14, which relate to the mining industry;

- Hazardous waste treatment, storage, or disposal facilities;

- Landfills, land application sites, and open dumps that receive or have received wastes from facilities considered to be engaged in industrial activity;

- Facilities involved in the recycling of materials, including metal scrap yards, battery reclaimers, salvage yards, and automobile junk yards;

- Steam electric power generating facilities;

- Transportation facilities that have vehicle maintenance shops, equipment cleaning operations, or airport deicing operations with respect to the areas of the facility where those operations are performed;

- Treatment works treating domestic sewage or any other sewage sludge or wastewater treatment device or system, used in the storage, treatment, recycling, and reclamation of municipal or domestic sewage with a design flow of 1.0 mgd or more, or required to have an approved pretreatment program under 40 CFR Part 403;

- Construction activity including clearing, grading, and excavation activities except operations that result in the disturbance of less than five acres of total land area, which are not a part of a larger common plan of development or sale; and

- Facilities within SIC codes 20, 21, 22, 23, 2434, 25, 265, 267, 27, 283, 285, 30, 31 (except 311), 323, 34 (except 3441), 35, 36, 37 (except 373), 38, 39, 4221-25 which are not included in the other categories listed above.

The KPDES permit requirement is applicable to storm water discharges from the categories of industrial activities listed above, except those identified in the final category, when the discharge is from: (1) industrial plant yards; (2) immediate access roads and rail lines used or traveled by carriers of raw materials, manufactured products, wastes or by-products used or created by the facility; (3) material handling sites; (4) refuse sites; (5) sites used for the application or disposal of process waste waters; (6) sites used for the storage and maintenance of material handling equipment; (7) sites used for residual treatment, storage, or disposal; (8) shipping and receiving areas; (9) manufacturing buildings; (10) storage areas, including tank farms, for raw materials and intermediate and finished products; and (11) areas where industrial activity has taken place in the past and significant materials remain. Discharges from these areas are subject to permitting without regard to whether pollutants are exposed to storm water in such areas. Storm water discharges from industrial activities in the SIC codes listed in the final category above are subject to the KPDES permit requirement only where material handling equipment or activities, raw materials, intermediate products, final products, waste materials, by-products, or industrial machinery are exposed to storm water.

For purposes of KPDES permit applicability, material handling activities include the storage, loading and unloading, transportation, or conveyance of any raw material, intermediate product, finished product, by-product, or waste product. However, storm water discharges from areas that are located at the facility but which are separate from the industrial activities, such as office buildings and parking lots are not subject to the KPDES permit requirement as long as the drainage from those areas does not combine with the storm water from the industrial activities at the site.

Under the Clean Water Act uncontaminated runoff from oil and gas operations is exempt from storm water permitting.[18] USEPA regulations provide that the discharge of storm water runoff from oil and gas exploration, production, processing, or treatment operations or

---

18 33 U.S.C. Section 1342 (l)(2)

transmission facilities is not subject to permitting if the discharge is composed entirely of: (1) flows from conveyances used for collecting and conveying precipitation runoff; and (2) that are not contaminated by contact with or that have not come into contact with any overburden, raw material, intermediate products, finished products, by-products, or wastes.[19] Storm water discharges that are contaminated are subject to the permit requirement. Under the federal regulation only oil and gas facilities that have had a release of a reportable quantity of oil or hazardous substances in storm water since November 16, 1987 and/or the facilities that contribute to a violation of a water quality standard, are required to submit a permit application.

Eight KPDES general permits have been issued authorizing the discharge of storm water associated with industrial activity. The permits apply to the following categories:

- construction activities
- landfills and land application
- coal pile runoff
- primary metals
- oil and gas exploration and production
- miscellaneous industrial activities
- wood preserving - creosote
- wood preserving - arsenic and chromium

Owners or operators of facilities that seek coverage under a general KPDES storm water discharge permit must submit a Notice of Intent to the Division of Water. Coverage under the permit commences 48 hours after submission of the Notice unless the Director of the Division

---

[19] 40 CFR 122.26(a)(2)

denies coverage and requires an individual permit application. If the discharge associated with industrial activity is through a separate municipal storm water system, the owner or operator must also submit the Notice to the municipality.

The KPDES general permits for storm water discharges do not impose numeric effluent limitations except for the general permit applicable to coal pile runoff. Instead, the KPDES general permits for storm water discharges require the development and implementation of storm water best management practice plans. Additionally, the permits impose requirements for the monitoring of effluent quality and the retention of monitoring records. The general KPDES permit for discharges from construction activity contains no effluent limitations or monitoring requirements but relies exclusively upon storm water best management practice plans.

Storm water best management practice plans form the backbone of the storm water KPDES permit program. Such plans require the development of an inventory of potential pollutant sources that may be exposed to storm water and an evaluation of drainage areas that may convey pollutants to surface waters. As part of the plan, the owner or operator must specify control programs such as spill prevention and response, site inspections, employee training and good housekeeping practices that are to be utilized to control storm water discharges. Qualified personnel must perform site investigations at least annually in order to confirm that the plan is performing its designed role. Storm water best management practices plans for construction activity must include several additional elements.

B. In-stream Water Quality Standards

The NREPC Division of Water has promulgated water quality standards that establish minimum in-stream conditions that must be attained in all surface waters in Kentucky. The

Kentucky water quality standards may be enforced directly against sources that cause or contribute to violations of the standards or indirectly through KPDES permits that include water quality-based effluent limitations. The Kentucky water quality standards are not applicable to groundwater.

Kentucky's water quality standards are codified in administrative regulations 401 KAR 5:026; 401 KAR 5:029; 401 KAR 5:030; and 401 KAR 5:031. The standards have been approved by USEPA except for limited provisions of 401 KAR 5:030.

401 KAR 5:026 designates the uses for which waters of Kentucky are to be protected. The uses for which streams may be designated are warm water aquatic habitat, cold water aquatic habitat, primary contact recreation, secondary contact recreation, domestic water supply, and outstanding state resource water. The regulation identifies a number of specific stream segments and the uses for which they are to be protected and designates all other stream segments for use as warm water aquatic habitat, primary contact recreation, secondary contact recreation, and domestic water supply. The default designation of all surface waters in Kentucky for warm water aquatic habitat use is a more protective use designation than is applicable in most other states.

Administrative regulation 401 KAR 5:029 establishes the state's policy regarding anti-degradation and the use of mixing zones and zones of initial dilution in calculation of water quality-based effluent limitations. Although environmental interest groups have challenged the validity of Kentucky's mixing zone/zones of initial dilution regulation on several occasions, the regulation has been upheld as consistent with the Clean Water Act and KRS Chapter 224.[20]

---

[20] Hackett v. NREPC, City of Emmience (Franklin Circuit Ct. 96-CI-1148; 1997)

401 KAR 5:030 was promulgated in 1995 to establish implementation procedures for the anti-degradation policy of 401 KAR 5:029. The regulation categorizes surface waters of Kentucky into three groups for anti-degradation purposes. The outstanding national resource water category consists of those waters that are of such unique quality or status that virtually no permanent pollutant loading may be added. The exceptional water category consists of waters having quality exceeding the minimum water quality standards and possessing excellent biological communities. Only limited additional pollutant loading from new and expanded sources is permitted in exceptional waters. The use-protected water category is comprised of all waters not designated as outstanding national resource waters or exceptional waters. Additional pollutant loading is permitted in use-protected waters as long as minimum water quality standards are satisfied and all designated uses are protected.

401 KAR 5:030 assigns specific stream segments to the various categories of anti-degradation protection. All stream segments that are not assigned to an anti-degradation category are, by default, categorized as use-protected waters. Approximately 3% of Kentucky's surface

waters are categorized as outstanding national resource waters or exceptional waters and approximately 97% are categorized as use-protected waters.

Designation of a stream segment as an exceptional water under 401 KAR 5:030 can severely limit future social and economic development on the stream segment. Under the regulation new and expanded discharges to such streams are, with certain exceptions, limited to one-half of the pollutant discharge that would otherwise be allowable.

In August 2000 USEPA disapproved the provisions of 401 KAR 5:030 that prescribe the criteria for re-designation of use-protected waters to the exceptional water category. USEPA asserted that the biological criteria utilized by the state agency for identification of exceptional waters were inconsistent with federal regulations requiring such protection to be afforded to all streams having water quality better than the minimum water quality standards. The NREPC Division of Water advised USEPA that it did not expect to satisfy the federal objections and that USEPA should proceed with promulgation of replacement federal standards if the federal agency deemed such action necessary.

401 KAR 5:031 establishes the criteria that apply to the various use designations identified under 401 KAR 5:026 and establishes certain additional criteria that are applicable to all surface waters without regard to their designated use. Most of the criteria in 401 KAR 5:031 are numeric; however, certain of the criteria are narrative. The regulation establishes criteria for the protection of aquatic life from both chronic and acute toxic effects. The regulation also prescribes the stream flow to be utilized in the development of water quality-based KPDES permit limitations. Although most of the criteria apply to all streams designated for the particular use, the criteria for the protection of domestic water supply apply only at the point of withdrawal for use. The regulation contains various provisions allowing exceptions to criteria where they are not necessary for the protection of the designated use and for specific individual discharges where enforcement of the standard would cause substantial and widespread adverse economic and social impact.

C. Non-Federal Water Quality Programs

Although most of the regulatory programs administered by the NREPC Division of Water are designed to implement the provisions of the Clean Water Act, some of its regulatory programs have no federal counterparts. These state-developed programs include the following:

- 401 KAR 5:005 - Permits for Wastewater Facilities

This regulation establishes a permit program to control the construction and operation of wastewater facilities other than industrial facilities which discharge pursuant to a KPDES permit. The primary focus of the program is the control of publicly owned treatment works, sanitary sewers and related facilities. The program also regulates through issuance of Kentucky No Discharge Operational Permits (KNDOP) industrial wastewater facilities that are exempt from the KPDES permit program such as closed-circuit coal washers, industrial spray irrigation and land spreading systems and certain animal feed lots.

- 401 KAR 5:090 - Water Pollution From Oil and Gas Facilities

This regulatory program was implemented in the early 1980s to address the effects of oil and gas production operations on Kentucky's waterways. All oil and gas production facilities that have the potential to generate produced water are subject to the regulation except that gas wells producing less than one barrel of water daily are exempt from most of the requirements. The regulation requires the registration and placarding of storage tanks and other facilities, restricts the transportation and off-site disposal of produced water, requires compliance with the KPDES permit program and in-stream water quality standards, controls the construction and operation of holding pits, limits the operation of drilling pits and limits the use of disposal wells.

- 401 KAR 5:037 - Groundwater Protection

In 1994 the NREPC Division of Water promulgated 401 KAR 5:037 to establish a comprehensive program to prevent the contamination of Kentucky's groundwater resources. Although the regulation is very broad in scope, it is limited to the prevention of groundwater contamination and does not address remediation of groundwater contamination after it has occurred. The regulation applies to persons who engage in any of the following activities and who do not qualify for exemption under the regulation:

- storage of bulk quantities of pesticides or fertilizers for commercial purposes or for distribution to retail outlets;
- application of pesticides or fertilizers for commercial purposes or for public right-of-way maintenance or institutional care;
- land treatment or land disposal of pollutants;
- management of wastes;
- commercial or industrial handling of bulk quantities of raw materials or intermediate or finished products in tanks, drums, containers or pits;
- pipeline transportation of materials, products or pollutants;
- storage, handling or application of road oils, dust suppressants or deicing agents;
- mining and associated activities;
- construction, operation and abandonment of wells and bore holes;
- use of floor drains that do not lead to KPDES-permitted outfalls;
- impoundment of pollutants in pits, ponds or lagoons;
- transfer of bulk quantities of raw materials, products or pollutants.

Since the applicability of 401 KAR 5:037 is not limited to specific substances or to specific quantities of materials, the scope of the regulation is potentially very broad. The following specific activities are, however, exempted from applicability of the regulation:

- retail marketing and normal use or consumption of products packaged for personal use by individuals;
- activities conducted entirely inside buildings having inpervious floors and no unregulated floor drains;
- the pipeline transmission of gaseous pollutants;

- the use of solid waste dumpsters;
- operation of sewer lines approved by NREPC;
- water storage;
- deicing of roads and parking lots;
- emergency response and fire-fighting activities;
- transportation of material by motor vehicle, rolling stock or aircraft; and
- agricultural activities including commercial fertilizer application at agricultural operations.

In addition to these specific exemptions, the regulation has a general exemption for persons who can demonstrate that the activity which they conduct has no reasonable potential to contaminate groundwater resources. The general exemption plays a key role in the regulatory structure since the fact that the program is not limited by substance or quantity would otherwise give the program unlimited applicability. The demonstration necessary to qualify for the general exemption is not required to be provided to or approved by the administering agency except upon request.

The basic element of Kentucky's groundwater regulatory program is the requirement that sources subject to the program prepare and implement a groundwater protection plan (GPP). A GPP is comparable to the storm water best management practices plan except that it applies to groundwater rather than storm water. GPP can be developed for individual facilities or as a generic plan applicable to a broad category of facilities.

GPP are required to address the physical facility, the activities that necessitate preparation of the plan, the practices to be implemented to protect groundwater, the schedule by which the practices are to be implemented, and an employee training and inspection schedule to insure adherence to the plan. Each GPP must bear a certification by the person responsible for its implementation that the plan complies with the regulation, that the person has reviewed the plan, and that the person will implement its provisions.

The GPP requirement of 401 KAR 5:037 is enforced under procedures similar to the spill prevention control and countermeasure plan (SPCC) requirement of 40 CFR Part 112. The GPP must be developed by the regulated entity and retained at the site available for inspection. The GPP does not have to be submitted to the NREPC Division of Water for review and approval except upon request. The GPP must be revised to reflect changes in the facility and must be reviewed and re-certified in its entirety at least every three years. Although no public participation is required for the development and implementation of GPP, the GPP must be made available for public inspection upon request. Upon the sale of property for which a GPP has been prepared, the seller must provide to the purchaser a copy of the most recent GPP.

- 401 KAR 5:200 - Five-Mile Water Policy

The NREPC Division of Water has adopted a policy which has regulatory effect that limits the construction of new or the expansion of existing wastewater discharges within five miles upstream of a public water supply intake. The policy includes a procedure for the issuance of variances from the prohibition. In order to qualify for a variance from the prohibition, the potential discharger must conduct a study to establish that the new or expanded discharge will not significantly affect water quality at the point of intake.

- KRS Chapter 224 Subchapter 71

KRS Chapter 224 Subchapter 71 establishes a special regulatory program to address the impact of agricultural operations on Kentucky's water quality. The statute establishes the Agriculture Water Quality Authority, an administrative agency attached to NREPC, to oversee the program. Under the program statewide and regional water quality plans are to be developed subject to the review and approval of NREPC Division of Water.

Under the statute individual agriculture operations of ten acres or more must establish and implement agriculture water quality plans consistent with the statewide and regional water quality plans. The statute includes special procedures for the enforcement of the requirements of the agriculture water quality plan involving notice to the agriculture operation and opportunity to remedy any non-compliance without formal enforcement action.

D. Safe Drinking Water Act

The Federal Safe Drinking Water Act (SDWA)[21] also forms the basis for certain environmental law programs in Kentucky. Under the SDWA, national drinking water standards are promulgated to protect public health and welfare from the adverse impact of contaminated drinking water. The NREPC Division of Water has been delegated responsibility for administration of the SDWA drinking water protection program and conducts it through administrative regulations that appear in 401 KAR Chapter 8.

The regulations implementing the SDWA drinking water protection program include standards for the operation and maintenance of water supply systems for public and semi-public use. Private water supply systems are not subject to SDWA regulation.

Another significant regulatory program under the SDWA is the Underground Inspection Control (UIC) program which is established under 40 CFR Parts 144 through 148. The purpose of the UIC program is to protect underground sources of drinking water from contamination

[21] 42 U.S.C. Section 300 f. et seq.

resulting from the injection of fluids through wells. The UIC program in Kentucky is administered by USEPA Region IV in Atlanta and its administration has not been delegated to Kentucky.

Wells that are subject to the UIC program include disposal wells, enhanced recovery wells used in oil and gas production, certain septic tanks and cesspools, and any other penetration to the sub-surface where the depth is greater than the widest surface dimension. Wells that are exempt from regulation under the UIC program include septic tanks and cesspools that serve fewer than twenty persons per day and injection wells used for storage of natural gas.

Under USEPA's UIC program regulations wells subject to the program are divided into five classes with different regulatory requirements applicable to each class. In Kentucky most wells that are subject to the UIC program are Class II wells utilized in the oil and gas production industry or Class V wells such as storm drainage wells, air conditioning re-injection wells, or septic tanks and cesspools that are not included in any other category.

Under the UIC program most existing wells are regulated through a permit-by-rule process while most new wells must obtain permits from USEPA in advance of their construction and operation. The UIC program prohibits the injection of fluids through wells if it will result in the movement of contaminants into an underground source of drinking water.

Technical standards for wells are established under 40 CFR Part 146. The technical standards require compliance with the following obligations:

- construction requirements;
- plugging and abandonment requirements;
- mechanical integrity testing requirements; and
- operating, monitoring and reporting requirements.

CHAPTER 4

Wetlands, Floodplain Compliance and Water Obstruction Regulations

A. Floodplain Construction

Pursuant to NREPC administrative regulation 401 KAR 4:060, construction in certain floodways is limited. Regulated floodways include a stream channel and that portion of adjacent land area required to pass flood flows without raising the base flood crest by more than one foot, except that in urban areas the backwater effect may be less than one foot. Floodway boundaries are determined by NREPC with a preferred determination based on the base flood flow frequency curve obtained from the U.S. Geological Survey, Water Resources Division or the U.S. Army Corps of Engineers.

Prohibited uses include any fill, deposit, obstruction, excavation, storage of materials, or structure that could adversely affect the efficiency or capacity of a regulated floodway, including structures that are designed for human habitation; associated with high flood damage potential; or not connected with permit or open space uses; and structures consistent with open space uses but which could obstruct flood flow.

Certain activities are permitted in a regulated floodway including the following:

- open space uses having no appreciable flood damage potential such as those associated with agriculture, silviculture, recreation, parking, storage yards, and certain sand and gravel operations;

- certain structures related to allowable open spaces if designed, constructed and placed so as to offer minimum obstruction to flood flows;

- structures necessary for navigation and waterborne freight handling and utility crossings, provided NREPC determines efforts have been made to reduce the impact these facilities have on flooding;

- dredging or removal of materials from between stream banks with disposal outside of the floodway;
- activities exempt under 401 KAR 4:020 and 4:050.

Authorized construction in a regulated floodplain must be performed in accordance with regulatory standards.

All new construction and substantial improvements of residential structures must have the lowest floor, including the basement, elevated to at least the base flood level or above if the local government has more stringent requirements, or be designed so that below the base flood level the structure is properly flood-proofed with walls substantially impermeable to the passage of water. Upon completion of the lowest floor, certification prepared by a registered land surveyor or professional engineer of the elevation of the lowest floor must be provided to the NREPC Division of Water. The Division of Water reviews the floor elevation survey and any deficiencies detected must be corrected by the permit holder immediately and prior to further work. All manufactured homes (mobile homes) must be elevated and properly anchored to resist flotations, collapse, or lateral movement. Non-residential structures may be approved if they are elevated to at least the base floodplain or if they are flood-proofed in accordance with the regulation.

The regulations recognize certain variances and exceptions from the construction prohibition. NREPC may allow an encroachment that causes a backwater effect if the applicant owns the entire subject property on both sides of the stream and NREPC has assurances by zoning or deed restrictions that none of the applicant's property will be subdivided and sold. NREPC may redesignate a regulatory floodway boundary on one side of the stream provided a permanent flooding easement is provided for the compensating area on the opposite side.

Additionally, NREPC may impose any other conditions it deems necessary to offset potential adverse flooding effects.

B. Dam Construction

Pursuant to KRS 151.250, no person, or city, county or other political subdivision of the Commonwealth of Kentucky may begin the construction, reconstruction, relocation or improvement of any dam, embankment, levee, dike, bridge, fill or other obstruction across any stream or any building, barrier, or obstruction adjacent to a river or stream in a floodway without approval by NREPC. However, ditches or systems established for agricultural purposes are exempt.

The minimum criteria for dams are established at 401 KAR 4:030. The Division of Water Engineering Memorandum No. 5 is incorporated by reference into the regulations and sets forth design requirements for spillways, earth embankments, utilities under embankments, and other such structures. The memorandum is available from the Division of Water upon request. Any structure type not generally used in Kentucky – including gravity, buttress, steel, or timber – will be considered on a case-by-case basis. The safety of the structure in relation to property and human life is the principal factor considered by the agency.

401 KAR 4:050 sets forth construction exemptions including an exemption for construction in or along a stream whose watershed is less than one square mile and for subfluvial utility or pipeline crossings that meet the criteria.

General provisions of the stream construction permits set forth in 401 KAR 4:060 include the use of best engineering practices, public notification of stream construction, and notice to

NREPC. Plans and specifications submitted for consideration must bear the seal and signature of the responsible engineer as defined in KRS 322.010(2).

Construction of dams, embankments, levees, dikes, bridges, fills and other stream obstructions proposed in conjunction with surface and deep mining are governed by the surface mining standards imposed by the NREPC Division of Surface Mine Reclamation, and are exempt from the provisions of KRS Chapter 151. (See 401 KAR 4:040.)

C. Discharge of Dredged or Fill Material

Section 404 of the Clean Water Act[22] regulates the discharge of dredged or fill material into waters of the United States by prohibiting such discharges in the absence of a permit issued by the U.S. Army Corps of Engineers. Regulations governing the operation of the program are codified in 33 CFR Parts 320 through 330. Waters within the scope of the program include those used for interstate commerce; interstate waters, intrastate lakes, rivers, streams (including intermittent streams), impoundments and tributaries of such waters; and adjacent wetlands the use or degradation of which could affect interstate commerce.

Corps of Engineers regulations exempt certain types of discharges from the permitting requirement including those from normal farming operations; maintenance and reconstruction of instream structures such as bridge abutments, dikes, and dams; and construction or maintenance of farm roads, forest roads, or temporary roads for moving mining equipment.

Pursuant to 33 CFR Part 330 certain types of activities that are required to be conducted under a Section 404 permit are authorized to be conducted under a nationwide permit. A

---

22 33 U.S.C. Section 1344

nationwide permit is a type of general permit issued by the Corps of Engineers to regulate, with little delay or paperwork, activities having minimal environmental impact. Presently relatively simple construction activities have been authorized under general permits including such activities as backfilling utility lines, minor road crossings, and discharges into head waters and isolated waters. Nationwide permits are subject to notification requirements and standard conditions set forth in 33 CFR Part 330. Certain activities also may be authorized under regional permits that are a form of general permit issued at the regional rather than national level.

If the work is covered by certain Corps of Engineers nationwide permits, an applicant must submit a request for certification of the project to the Division of Water. The applicant is required to submit the completed application form along with a detailed description of the proposed action, location maps, detailed plans/drawings/specifications, and a copy of the Corps letter to the applicant authorizing the activity under a nationwide permit.

Activities that are not authorized under a nationwide or regional permit must be authorized under an individual Section 404 permit. Applications for Section 404 permits are reviewed for an evaluation of the impact of the proposed action on the public interest. Factors that are to be considered in the review of applications for Section 404 permits include the benefit from the proposed activity and its reasonably foreseeable detriments, conservation, wetland protection, impact on historical properties, fish and wildlife values, navigation, recreation, safety, and a variety of other interests. Corps of Engineers Section 404 permits must be consistent with EPA guidelines including specific procedures for the protection of wetlands.

CHAPTER 5

Air Quality

The federal Clean Air Act[23] forms the foundation for practically all regulation of air quality and air emission sources in Kentucky. Clean Air Act programs are administered in Kentucky under broad program standards established by USEPA and implemented by the NREPC Division for Air Quality (DAQ) under the federalism concept. These programs include ambient air quality standards that specify the air quality goals applicable to the air to which the general public is exposed; implementation plans that specify the measures to be taken to achieve the ambient air quality standards; and various emission standards that apply without regard to ambient air quality considerations. The Clean Air Act regulatory programs are enforced through a federal operating permit program administered by DAQ in conjunction with a state-developed construction/operating permit program.

A. Federal Clean Air Act Provisions

Title I of the Clean Air Act[24] provides the statutory underpinning for a large part of the basic air pollution control programs. Section 107[25] of the Clean Air Act directs each state to delineate air quality control regions within the state and to designate each such air quality control

---

23 42 U.S.C. 7401 et. seq.

24 42 U.S.C. 7401 et. seq.

25 42 U.S.C. 7407

region as to its status of compliance with ambient air quality standards. Sections 108[26] and 109[27] provide for USEPA promulgation of criteria for specific air pollutants and national ambient air quality standards for such pollutants at levels protective of public health and welfare. Section 110[28] requires the development of state implementation plans subject to federal review and approval that will result in attainment of the national ambient air quality standards. Section 111[29] establishes a program for imposition of technology-based new source performance standards applicable to certain categories of new and modified sources of air pollution. Section 112[30] provides for the control of emissions of hazardous air pollutants pursuant to standards established for various categories of sources. Sections 160 through 170[31] establish the prevention of significant deterioration (PSD) program to protect the quality of air resources that are better than national ambient air quality standards through a permit program for major new and modified sources based upon allowable increments of air quality impact and application of best available control technology (BACT). Sections 171 through 193[32] provide control programs for areas that are in non-attainment with national ambient air quality standards including emission offset and lowest achievable emission rate (LAER) pollution control technology requirements for major

[26] 42 U.S.C. 7408

[27] 42 U.S.C. 7409

[28] 42 U.S.C. 7410

[29] 42 U.S.C. 7411

[30] 42 U.S.C. 7412

[31] 42 U.S.C. 7470 et seq.

[32] 42 U.S.C. 7501 et seq.

new and modified sources in such areas along with mandatory control procedures designed to achieve compliance with the standards.

Other titles of the Clean Air Act address the following subjects:

- Title II[33] provides for control of mobile sources of air pollutants primarily through nationally-applicable tailpipe emission controls for vehicles and fuel quality standards developed to protect vehicle air pollution control equipment;

- Title III[34] establishes general provisions for the administration of the Clean Air Act;

- Title IV[35] creates the acid rain control program limiting the emission of sulfur and nitrogen oxides from large fuel combustion units;

- Title V[36] establishes an operating permit program applicable to major sources of air pollutants similar to the NPDES permit program for water discharges; and

- Title VI[37] provides for the regulation of substances that have the potential to deplete the ozone layer.

B. State Air Pollution Control Statutes

Kentucky's programs to control air pollution are based primarily upon administrative regulations rather than statutes. The statutes that relate to air pollution control include the following:

- KRS 224.10-100 authorizes NREPC to prevent, control and abate air pollution and to issue permits for the construction and operation of sources of air pollution.

---

33 42 U.S.C. 7521 et seq.

34 42 U.S.C. 7601 et seq.

35 42 U.S.C. 7651 et seq

36 42 U.S.C. 7661 et seq.

37 42 U.S.C. 7671 et seq.

The statue also authorizes NREPC to administer the Clean Air Act prevention of significant deterioration (PSD) program in a manner no more stringent than the federal program;

- KRS 224.20-050 through KRS 224.20-130 specifies the legislative findings as to the necessity for the implementation of the air pollution control program and the factors to be considered by NREPC in its establishment of standards. Additionally, these statutory provisions prohibit emissions that cause or contribute to air pollution, provide for concurrent jurisdiction of NREPC and local air pollution districts within the geographic boundaries of such districts, and provide for the imposition of emission fees to support administration of the Clean Air Act Title V operating permit program;

- KRS 224.20-300 through KRS 224.20-320 creates a state asbestos control program to implement the federal Asbestos Hazard Emergency Response Act[38];

- KRS 224.20-500 through KRS 224.20-515 establishes a small business stationary source advisory program to assist small businesses in their efforts to comply with Clean Air Act requirements;

- KRS 224.20-710 through KRS 224.20-765 establishes a vehicle emission testing program to carry out Clean Air Act program requirements; and

- KRS Chapter 77 provides for the creation of local air pollution control districts and their development and implementation of standards and regulations subject to the review and approval of NREPC. Such local air pollution control requirements must be at least as stringent as comparable state air pollution control requirements and the state and local air pollution control agencies exercise concurrent jurisdiction within the geographic area encompassed by the local district. The only local air pollution control district that is currently active is the Air Pollution Control District of Jefferson County (APCDJC).

C. Air Pollution Control Regulations

Pursuant to Section 107 of the Clean Air Act[39], the NREPC Division for Air Quality (DAQ) through administrative regulation 401KAR 50:020 has subdivided Kentucky into nine air

---

[38] 15 U.S.C. 2641 et seq.

[39] 42 U.S.C. 7407

quality control regions of which five are interstate regions including parts of other states. The designation of areas as to their status of attainment of ambient air quality standards has been implemented by county rather than by air quality control region. Administrative regulation 401 KAR 51:010 identifies the counties and parts of counties as to their attainment status. Most Kentucky counties have been designated as attainment for all pollutants or are in the process of being so designated. The principal exception involves USEPA's recently-promulgated 8-hour ozone standard. For that standard as few as 18 counties or as many as 33 counties may be designated as non-attainment. No designations have been made for USEPA's recently-promulgated $PM_{2.5}$ standard.

USEPA has implemented Sections 108[40] and 109[41] of the Clean Air Act by establishing in 40 CFR Part 50 national ambient air quality standards for sulfur dioxide, particulate matter, carbon monoxide, ozone, nitrogen dioxide and lead. In July 1997 USEPA adjusted its ambient air quality standards by establishing a standard for fine particulates ($PM_{2.5}$) and an eight-hour standard for ozone. These standards have been challenged in federal court proceedings and have not been fully implemented.

DAQ has promulgated in 401 KAR Chapter 53 state ambient air quality standards comparable to those promulgated by USEPA (except for the $PM_{2.5}$ and 8-hour ozone standards). DAQ has also promulgated state ambient air quality standards for hydrogen sulfide, fluorides and odor that have no federal counterparts. Under 401 KAR Chapter 53, the state ambient air quality standards, unlike their federal counterparts, are independently enforceable against persons who

---

[40] 42 U.S.C. 7408

[41] 42 U.S.C. 7409

cause or contribute to violations of the standards. The state ambient air quality standard for odor is somewhat unique in that it applies only to situations in which an odor complaint has been lodged with NREPC.

Pursuant to Section 110[42] of the Clean Air Act, DAQ has developed and USEPA has approved state implementation plans (SIP) for those areas of Kentucky that have been designated nonattainment for various pollutants. In Jefferson County, the SIP has been developed by APCDJC.

The Kentucky SIP consists primarily of administrative regulations establishing emission limitations designed to achieve compliance with ambient air quality standards. Accordingly, many of the regulations apply only to specific types of activities or specific geographic areas. Other regulations apply generally without being tailored to achieve specific air quality objectives. Kentucky's SIP regulations are codified in 401 KAR Chapters 51 (regulating new and modified sources under the PSD and nonattainment new source review programs); 59 and 60 (establishing standards for new sources); 61 (establishing standards for existing sources); 63 (general standards); and 65 (vehicle emission testing).

Although USEPA has approved the Kentucky SIP, the federal agency has, from time-to-time, required the state to revise or update the SIP to reflect new air quality data or changes in federal requirements for SIP. Most recently, USEPA has required states including Kentucky to regulate through SIP revisions emissions of nitrous oxides primarily from large fuel burning facilities such as electric utility generating units and large industrial boilers. SIPs have not yet

---

[42] 42 U.S.C. 7410

been required for the newly-promulgated eight-hour ozone standard or the $PM_{2.5}$ fine particulate standard.

Pursuant to Section 111[43] of the Clean Air Act USEPA has promulgated in 40 CFR Part 60 new source performance standards (NSPS) applicable to approximately 77 categories of new and modified stationary sources. These regulations establish technology-based limitations that constitute minimum requirements applicable to such categories. The requirements apply to each new or modified affected facility subject to such standards and sources are not permitted to achieve compliance by over-controlling other affected facilities within the source. Compliance with the new source performance standards is required at the time of start-up of the new or modified affected facility although the source is afforded a short period of operation to reach normal production levels and to conduct performance tests demonstrating compliance.

The NREPC Division for Air Quality has promulgated administrative regulations in 401 KAR Chapters 59 and 60 to implement the federal Clean Air Act NSPS. Most of the state regulations incorporate by reference the federal standards thereby obviating any issue as to the relative stringency of the state and federal standards. USEPA has delegated to NREPC primary responsibility for implementation of the Clean Air Act Section 111[44] NSPS.

Although Section 112[45] of the Clean Air Act had for many years authorized USEPA to regulate the emission of hazardous air pollutants, under national emission standards for hazardous air pollutants (NESHAP), USEPA had made little progress in the regulation of such

---

[43] 42 U.S.C. 7411

[44] 42 U.S.C. 7411

[45] 42 U.S.C. 7412

emissions by the time the Clean Air Act Amendments were enacted in 1990. Because of the cumbersome regulatory procedures of Section 112, only benzene, vinyl chloride, asbestos and a handful of other hazardous air pollutant emissions had been regulated by USEPA under standards codified in 40 CFR Part 61. The 1990 Clean Air Act Amendments established a program under which USEPA was to promulgate administrative regulations for numerous categories of sources of hazardous air pollutants requiring the application of maximum available control technology (MACT). Separate MACT standards are to be developed for existing sources and for new and reconstructed sources reflecting the different levels of technology available for such sources. Upon the completion of the MACT phase of hazardous air pollutant regulation, USEPA is required to evaluate the residual risk posed by hazardous air pollutant emissions and to develop an additional regulatory program to protect the public against exposure to any unacceptable residual risk.

USEPA has implemented Section 112 of the Clean Air Act as amended in 1990 by promulgating MACT standards for approximately 38 categories of hazardous air pollutant emission sources which are set forth in 40 CFR Part 63. USEPA has scheduled the promulgation of MACT standards for numerous additional categories prior to the 2002 statutory deadline.

MACT standards are generally applicable to major sources of hazardous air pollutants. Major sources are those which have the potential to emit at least 10 tons of a single hazardous air pollutant or at least 25 tons of hazardous air pollutants on an aggregate basis. Fugitive emissions must be included in the calculation of a source's potential to emit hazardous air pollutants. USEPA has the authority to extend specific MACT standards to non-major area sources of hazardous air pollutants but has generally limited MACT standard applicability to major sources.

The potential to emit hazardous air pollutants is determined on the basis of maximum production from the physical design of the facility. In many instances the potential to emit greatly exceeds actual emission levels if the operation is not conducted at maximum levels on an around-the-clock basis. Sources that have a potential to emit at major source levels that would trigger applicability of MACT standards may limit their potential to emit below major source levels by accepting federally enforceable limitations on such variables as hours of operation, amount of material processed, or level of production. Under USEPA policy, sources with a potential to emit hazardous air pollutants at major source levels may assume federally enforceable limitations and avoid applicability of MACT standards until the initial compliance date under the MACT standard. If, however, a source once becomes subject to MACT standards, the source cannot thereafter avoid applicability of MACT standards by accepting federally enforceable limitations and reducing its potential to emit.

Under Clean Air Act Section 112, existing sources must comply with applicable MACT standards within three years of promulgation of the standard. Under limited circumstances the deadline for compliance can be extended for an additional year. New and reconstructed sources subject to MACT standards must comply when they commence operation.

The NREPC Division for Air Quality has promulgated administrative regulations in Kentucky that are counterparts to USEPA's NESHAP regulations. The state regulations implementing USEPA's NESHAP regulations prior to enactment of the 1990 Clean Air Act Amendments are codified at 401 KAR Chapter 57:002. The Division's administrative regulations comparable to USEPA's MACT standards promulgated after enactment of the 1990 amendments appear at 401 KAR 63:002. Both 401 KAR 57:002 and 401 KAR 63:002 incorporate by reference the federal NESHAP regulations.

The 1990 Clean Air Act Amendments also added Section 112(r)[46] which provides for USEPA development of a regulatory program for chemical accident prevention and risk management. USEPA promulgated its Section 112(r) regulations effective July 1, 1998 and codified them at 40 CFR Part 68.

The purpose of the Clean Air Act Section 112(r) regulations at 40 CFR Part 68 is to encourage sources to reduce the probability of accidental release of substances that have the potential to cause immediate harm to public health and the environment and to stimulate a dialogue between industry and the public to improve accident prevention and emergency response procedures. The initial step in implementation of the program was the promulgation of administrative regulations establishing a list of regulated substances and threshold quantities defining the applicability of the program requirements.

On June 20, 1996, USEPA promulgated amendments to 40 CFR Part 68 imposing substantive requirements pursuant to Clean Air Act Section 112(r). The regulations divided sources subject to the regulation into three categories based on the potential for offsite consequences associated with a worst-case accidental release; accident history; and compliance with the prevention requirements of OSHA's process safety management standard. Processes having no potential impact on the public in case of an accidental release were assigned minimal requirements. For other processes, sources were required to implement a risk management program including more detailed requirements for hazard assessment, prevention and emergency response. Processes in industry categories with a history of accidental releases and processes that

---

[46] 42 U.S.C. 7412(r)

already comply with the OSHA process safety management standard were required to implement prevention programs parallel to the OSHA program requirements.

The basic element of 40 CFR Part 68 is the requirement for preparation of a risk management plan by sources subject to the regulation. The plan must include an analysis of off-site consequences of a worst-case release scenario. The plan must be submitted to the administering agency and be available to the public.

In Kentucky the Clean Air Act Section 112(r) chemical accident prevention and risk management program is implemented under administrative regulations promulgated by the NREPC Division for Air Quality. The state regulations became effective in October, 1999 and are codified at 401 KAR Chapter 68. The state regulations adopt by reference USEPA's Section 112(r) program regulations with specific exemptions for certain retail facilities selling flammable fuel or propane.

From 1986 until 1999, the NREPC Division for Air Quality administered a state program for the regulation of toxic air pollutant emissions separate and apart from Clean Air Act requirements. Kentucky's toxic air pollutant control program was implemented under administrative regulations 401 KAR 63:021 (existing sources) and 401 KAR 63:022 (new and modified sources). In 1999 the Division for Air Quality repealed 401 KAR 63:022 and amended 401 KAR 63:021 so that its only effect was to require sources that had been issued permits with conditions based on the state air toxics regulation to continue to comply with such conditions unless the source demonstrated that the conditions were no longer necessary to protect human health and the environment. The APCDJC adopted air toxics regulations similar to 401 KAR 63:021 and 401 KAR 63:022 which continue in effect in Jefferson County.

Although the Division for Air Quality's comprehensive toxic air pollutant regulatory program was repealed in 1999 except for the anti-backsliding provision of amended 401 KAR 63:021, a more general administrative regulation 401 KAR 63:020 addressing the emission of potentially hazardous matter or toxic substances continues in effect. 401 KAR 63:020 authorizes the Division to limit, on a case-by-case basis, emissions that are not otherwise regulated, if they are potentially harmful to the health and welfare of humans, plants and animals. 401 KAR 63:020 is implemented through permit conditions based upon risk assessment methodology.

D. Air Pollution Permit Requirements

Until enactment of the Clean Air Act Amendments of 1990 the Clean Air Act regulatory requirements were primarily implemented through emission standards or limitations directly enforced by USEPA or by authorized states rather than through a comprehensive permit program. Prior to the 1990 amendments, the only Clean Air Act regulatory requirements implemented through a permit program were the prevention of significant deterioration (PSD) program applicable to construction or major modification of major stationary sources in clean air areas and the nonattainment new source review (NSR) program applicable to construction or major modification of major stationary sources in areas that did not attain ambient air quality standards. Some states, such as Kentucky, had also developed state construction/operating permit programs as part of their SIPs under Section 110[47] of the Clean Air Act.

---

[47] 42 U.S.C. 7410

In 1990 Congress amended the Clean Air Act to add Title V[48] providing for a federal operating permit program comparable to the NPDES permit program for wastewater discharges. Unlike the PSD and NSR programs which provide mechanisms for the establishment of requirements through the issuance of permits, the Title V permit program is designed to accumulate in one document all of the applicable requirements of the source rather than to impose new or additional requirements. The Clean Air Act provides for delegation of Title V permit program implementation from USEPA to the states and provides for sanctions against states that fail to implement Title V permit program requirements.

USEPA's basic PSD permit program regulations were promulgated in August, 1980 and are codified at 40 CFR 51.166 (requirements for state programs) and 40 CFR 52.21 (requirements for federal programs). The regulations prohibit the construction or major modification of major stationary sources in areas that have attained compliance with national ambient air quality standards prior to the issuance of a PSD permit. The PSD status of a new source or major modification is determined by its potential to emit pollutants subject to PSD review. For purposes of PSD review, a major source is one that has the potential to emit more than 250 tons per year of a pollutant regulated under the Clean Air Act or that emits more than 100 tons per year of such pollutants if the source is in one of twenty-eight categories identified in the law and regulations. Lower thresholds apply to major modifications. Sources may avoid PSD review by accepting federally enforceable limitations on their operation to keep their potential to emit below major source or major modification thresholds. Sources that do so are referred to as synthetic minor sources or modifications.

---

[48] 42 U.S.C. 7661 et seq.

Major modifications of minor sources are not subject to PSD review unless the modification would itself constitute a major source for purposes of PSD review. Thus a change at an existing facility that causes a minor source to become a major source will not necessarily be subject to PSD review. The determination as to whether a modification triggers PSD review is based upon the calculation of contemporaneous net emission increases on a facility-wide basis. Such an evaluation normally involves consideration of emission increases and decreases that have taken place at the facility within the five years preceding the current change and affords the facility the opportunity to avoid PSD review by implementing emission reductions concurrently with the planned modification. Sources that avoid PSD review through contemporaneous emission reductions are said to have "netted out of review".

Certain changes are specifically exempt from consideration as modifications that would trigger PSD review. These changes include the following:

- Routine maintenance, repair and replacement;
- Use of alternative fuels or raw materials under limited circumstances;
- increase in hours of operation or production rate subject to specific limitations; and
- change in ownership;

Numerous controversies have arisen as to whether maintenance activities that significantly prolong the useful life of facilities constitute routine maintenance or repair that is exempt from PSD review.

Under the Clean Air Act and its implementing regulations, the requirements applicable to sources subject to PSD review include the following:

- installation of best available control technology (BACT) for all pollutants for which PSD review is triggered;

- emission of pollutants at levels that will not cause or contribute to violation of ambient air quality standards and that will be consistent with maintenance of prescribed air quality increments below the ambient air quality standards based upon air quality modeling; and

- protection of air quality in areas such as national parks and national wilderness that are designated as Class I areas.

PSD permits can only be issued after public notice and comment. Since the public notice and comment procedures and review of the technology and air quality impact issues can be time-consuming, persons seeking to undertake projects that are potentially subject to the PSD permit requirement frequently seek to avoid PSD review by qualifying as synthetic minor activities or netting out of review. USEPA has approved Kentucky's SIP for implementation of the PSD program in Kentucky. As a result of this approval, decision-making authority as to technology and air quality impact issues is vested in the NREPC DAQ rather than USEPA. The federal agency reviews permit actions by the state agency from a program oversight standpoint.

The NREPC DAQ has promulgated administrative regulation 401 KAR 51:017 to implement substantive aspects of the PSD program in Kentucky and 401 KAR 52:020 prescribing procedural aspects of the PSD permit process. Since KRS 224.10-100(26) provides that Kentucky's PSD regulations shall be "no more stringent than federal requirements", it is not surprising that state administrative regulation 401 KAR 51:017 is very similar to the federal PSD regulations at 40 CFR 51.166 and 40 CFR 52.21. One significant difference between the state and federal programs involves the contemporaneous timeframe for consideration of emission increases and decreases when netting out of PSD review. Unlike the federal program which takes into account emission increases and decreases that occur within five years of the proposed action, the state program takes into account changes that occur within ten years of the proposed action. For construction that commences after January 6, 2002, the state program will utilize a five year contemporaneous period comparable to the federal program.

In Jefferson County, PSD permit program requirements are codified in APCDJC Regulation 2.05. The local regulation is comparable to the state and federal PSD regulations but also includes a provision modifying the first-come first-served approach to PSD increment consumption by prohibiting the owner or operator of a PSD source from consuming an inordinate portion of the PSD air quality increment without the approval of the APCDJC Board.

The nonattainment new source review (NSR) permit program provided for by Section 173[49] of the Clean Air Act is similar in many respects to the PSD permit program; however, the NSR program applies to the construction of new major sources or the major modification of existing sources in areas that have not attained compliance with ambient air quality standards. Despite its similarity to PSD, the NSR permit program is significantly more stringent than PSD as to the level of air pollution control technology that must be utilized and as to the overall limitations on pollutant emissions to the atmosphere.

For purposes of NSR a major stationary source is one that has the potential to emit more than 100 tons per year of a pollutant for which the area is identified as nonattainment. The threshold for identification of major modifications under NSR is significantly lower than the new source threshold. Sources may avoid NSR by becoming synthetic minor sources or modifications through acceptance of federally enforceable limitations on hours of operation, production levels or materials utilized so as to lower the potential to emit below NSR threshold levels.

---

[49] 42 U.S.C. 7503

Under the NSR program, new and modified major sources must install lowest achievable emission rate (LAER) technology in lieu of the BACT technology that is required under the PSD program. LAER is the most stringent emission limitation that is contained in a SIP or that has been achieved in practice for such a category of sources anywhere in the country.

Under the NSR program any permit authorizing construction of a new major source or major modification in a nonattainment area must require the source to offset the increased emissions of the nonattainment pollutant by emission reductions from the same source or elsewhere within the nonattainment area. The emission offsets must be accomplished by the time the emissions from the new or modified source commence. The required ratio of offsetting emission reductions to new emissions varies depending upon the severity of the nonattainment problem in the area where the new or expanded facility is to be located.

Since new major sources have no existing operations from which to obtain the emission offsets required under the NSR program, the designation of an area as nonattainment can serve as a significant limiting factor on industrial development in the area. Some areas such as Jefferson County have developed emission reduction banking programs in an effort to accommodate further economic growth. The general effect of the Clean Air Act NSR program has been to steer economic development away from urban areas that are designated nonattainment under the Clean Air Act and toward less-urbanized areas that are designated attainment.

In Kentucky the nonattainment NSR program has been implemented by the NREPC Division for Air Quality by promulgation of administrative regulation 401 KAR 51:052. The NSR permit program in Kentucky is comparable to the program administered by USEPA under the Clean Air Act.

The addition of Title V[50] to the Clean Air Act in 1990 made a fundamental change in the role of federal permits in the administration of the Clean Air Act. Prior to enactment of Title V, federal permitting was required only for construction of new major stationary sources or major modification of existing major stationary sources. In contrast, Title V provided for regulation under a federal permit program delegated to authorized states of the operation of all major sources, both new and existing, and for the regulation of certain area sources that are subject to federal NSPS or NESHAP. The Title V permit program was modeled after the Clean Water Act NPDES permit program and was designed to allow all requirements applicable to a source to be identified by reference to a single document.

The scope of coverage of the Title V permit program was also broadened by definition of the term "major source" more expansively than it had been for purposes of other Clean Air Act programs such as PSD. Title V provides that a source is "major" and subject to the permit requirement if it has a potential to emit one hundred tons or more of any regulated pollutant, ten tons or more of a listed hazardous air pollutant or twenty-five tons or more of all hazardous air pollutants in the aggregate. For purposes of the Title V permit program, the potential to emit is determined on the basis of maximum operation under the physical design of the source. Sources desiring to avoid Title V applicability may lower the potential to emit below the threshold for applicability by accepting federally enforceable limitations on their operation. Sources that avoid Title V applicability through federally enforceable limitations on their potential to emit are referred to as conditional major sources.

---

[50] 42 U.S.C. 7661 et. seq.

The Title V permit program, like the NPDES permit program, authorizes the issuance of permits for a maximum term of five years. Permits are to be issued after public notice and comment by the public, by USEPA and by neighboring states. USEPA has the right to object to state-issued Title V permits and to issue its own permit to the source if the state fails to revise the permit to satisfy USEPA objections.

Section 504[51] of the Clean Air Act requires that all Title V permits contain enforceable emission limitations and standards, a schedule of compliance, a requirement that the results of mandated monitoring be submitted to USEPA and other conditions necessary to assure compliance. Section 504(f)[52] of the Clean Air Act provides a permit shield specifying that compliance with a Title V permit shall constitute compliance with Clean Air Act regulatory requirements that were properly identified in the source's Title V permit application.

USEPA has promulgated administrative regulations to carry out the Title V permit program that are codified at 40 CFR Part 70. Additional regulations at 40 CFR Part 71 establish a federal Title V permit to be implemented in the event that states fail to put in place a program under 40 CFR Part 70.

USEPA's 40 CFR Part 70 regulations supplement the Clean Air Act Title V statutory provisions in a number of respects including provisions on the following matters:

- deferral of Title V permit obligation for area sources subject to federal NSPS and NESHAP;
- inclusion of a phased schedule for the issuance of permits;
- requirements for submission of annual compliance certifications;

---

[51] 42 U.S.C. 7661C

[52] 42 U.s.C. 7661 C(f.)

- periodic monitoring obligations where the applicable requirement does not specify such an obligation;
- calculations for payment of emission fees to support Title V permit program administration;
- separation of state-origin requirements from federally-enforceable requirements;
- response to emergency situations;
- operational flexibility provisions authorizing off-permit changes and Section 502(b)10 changes without prior public notice and comment;
- a requirement that the permittee notify the permitting authority of deviations from the permit or other violations.

The NREPC DAQ received interim approval to administer the Title V permit program in December, 1995. The state's interim authority will expire in December, 2001 unless full approval is received prior to that time. The APCDJC received full approval to administer the Title V program in Jefferson County in April, 1996.

In Kentucky the issuance of permits to air pollution emission sources is conducted under administrative regulations set forth in 401 KAR Chapter 52. That chapter includes three principal regulations each of which prescribes procedures for the issuance of permits in certain types of situations. Each of the regulations addresses the permit procedures in general and incorporates by reference a document specifying the detailed procedures applicable to that type of permit.

401 KAR Chapter 52 includes the following regulations addressing a category of permit issued by the NREPC Division for Air Quality:

- 401 KAR 52:020 - This regulation provides for the state issuance of Title V permits and includes PSD permits and nonattainment NSR permits;

- 401 KAR 52:030 - This regulation provides for the state issuance of permits with federally enforceable limitations other than Title V permits. This regulation applies to permits for synthetic minor and conditional major sources; and

- 401 KAR 52:040 - This regulation applies to state-origin permits.

Permits issued by the NREPC Division for Air Quality under 401 KAR Chapter 52 are combined construction/operation permits. Accordingly, the same regulations address both the construction and the operation of sources within the category.

In January, 2001, NREPC DAQ made substantial revisions to its permit regulations. The issues addressed by the 2001 revisions include the following:

- separation of the previous regulation into separate regulations for each type of permit issued by the Division;

- relaxation of provisions so as to afford sources the operational flexibility to make off-permit changes, Section 502(b)(10) changes, and minor permit revisions without public notice and comment;

- deletion of authorization to add insignificant activities through administrative permit amendments;

- revision of compliance certification requirements; and

- adjustment of requirements applicable to state-origin sources.

In Jefferson County, APCDJC issues permits pursuant to Regulation 2. Title V permits are issued pursuant to Reg.2.16 while other permits, Federally Enforceable District Origin Operating Permits ("FEDOOP") are issued pursuant to Reg. 2.17. Other associated permit issuance requirements, e.g., PSD regulations and emission and permit fees, are also found within Regulation 2.

The APCDJC program is run pursuant to KRS Chapter 77 and therefore has a different statutory basis from the DAQ program. In most respects, the permit issuance process is very similar. However, because the APCDJC submits its own SIP revisions to USEPA for approval, there are frequently small, but potentially significant, differences between the state permitting regulations and Jefferson County regulations.

In addition, because Jefferson County has been nonattainment for ozone since standards were first promulgated, it has a long history of requiring Reasonably Available Control Technology ("RACT") of sources of VOC and NO_x emissions (Regulation 6.24 and 7.25). The agency has been requiring sources with RACT control plans to undergo public review and has submitted the plans to USEPA for review and inclusion in the SIP. Because of the difficulties associated with siting new sources or expanding existing sources in the nonattainment area, there is an active emissions trading system in Jefferson County that is operated pursuant to Regulation 2.12.

E. Other Air Pollution Control Programs

In addition to the broad Clean Air Act regulatory programs outlined above, the Act also establishes programs that apply to limited categories of activities. For example, Title IV[53] of the Clean Air Act as amended establishes the "acid rain" or "acid deposition" control program. USEPA has promulgated administrative regulations codified at 401 CFR Part 72 to carry out this program. Under this program electric utility generating units are subject to limitations on their emissions of sulfur oxides and nitrogen oxides. The requirements are imposed through control requirements and emission allocations on a plant-by-plant basis; however, compliance can be achieved through a cap-and-trade system for emission allocations designed to allow controls to be applied to those plants where it can be achieved in a more cost-effective manner.

---

[53] 42 U.S.C. 7651 et seq.

The NREPC Division for Air Quality has adopted by reference USEPA's 40 CFR Part 72 acid rain regulations. The state acid rain regulation is 401 KAR 50:072. The requirements of the acid rain program are enforced through conditions imposed in Title V permits.

The Clean Air Act also includes Title VI[54] which addresses stratospheric ozone protection. Title VI identifies a number of chlorofluorocarbon (CFC) substances the emissions of which have the potential to deplete the stratospheric ozone layer and establishes a program for the phase-out of their use. USEPA is authorized to promulgate regulations to carry out the statutory provisions. One of the major sources of CFC emissions has been from the servicing of air conditioning units on motor vehicles, appliances and industrial refrigeration units. The performance of such services has been regulated by USEPA to minimize the emission of CFCs since the early 1990s. USEPA has exclusive responsibility for administration of the stratospheric-ozone depletion program under Title VI and the NREPC Division for Air Quality is not directly involved in its administration. Since CFCs are pollutants regulated under the Clean Air Act, certain new and modified sources of CFC emissions are subject to regulation under the PSD program which is administered by the state agency.

In addition to the Clean Air Act programs, the NREPC DAQ also administers the asbestos assessment, response and accreditation program pursuant to the federal Asbestos Hazard Emergency Response Act (AHERA)[55] amendments to the Toxic Substances Control Act (TSCA). Implementation of the state asbestos program is authorized by KRS 224.20-300 and is

---

[54] 42 U.S.C. 7671 et seq.

[55] 15 U.S.C. 2641 et seq.

conducted pursuant to administrative regulations codified in 401 KAR Chapter 58 which also contains the Division's regulations implementing the federal asbestos NESHAP.

CHAPTER 6

Waste Management

The basic legal foundation for regulation of the management of wastes at the national level is the Resource Conservation and Recovery Act (RCRA)[56] which was enacted in 1976 as an amendment to the Solid Waste Disposal Act.[57] Subtitle C of RCRA[58] provided for the establishment of a federal program for cradle-to-grave regulation of hazardous waste to be developed by USEPA and administered by authorized states. In regard to non-hazardous wastes Subtitle D of RCRA[59] provided for the development of federal guidelines for the disposal of solid wastes and promulgation by USEPA of criteria for sanitary landfills and open dumps; however, primary responsibility for the regulation of non-hazardous wastes was left with state governments. RCRA also added Section 7003[60] to the Solid Waste Disposal Act authorizing USEPA to initiate legal actions to address any imminent and substantial endangerment to health or the environment that might arise from the past or present management of any solid waste or hazardous waste.

---

[56] Pub. L. 94-580

[57] 42 U.S.C. 6901 et seq.

[58] 42 U.S.C. 6921 et seq.

[59] 42 U.S.C. 6941 et seq.

[60] 42 U.S.C. 6973

The Solid Waste Disposal Act was also amended in 1980 by enactment of the Used Oil Recycling Act[61] and in 1984 by the enactment of the Hazardous and Solid Waste Amendments Act (HSWA)[62]. HSWA included provisions establishing minimum technology requirements for hazardous waste land disposal units, providing for corrective action at facilities required to obtain hazardous waste permits, and comprehensively regulating underground storage tanks for petroleum and hazardous substances.

A. Hazardous Waste Regulation

Although the RCRA legislation was enacted in 1976, administrative regulations establishing the cradle-to-grave hazardous waste regulatory program were not promulgated until May 19, 1980 and did not become effective until November 19, 1980. Under USEPA's interpretation of RCRA, hazardous wastes that were not actively managed after the November 19, 1980 effective date of the RCRA hazardous waste regulations are not subject to Subtitle C regulatory requirements.

Subtitle C of RCRA provides for USEPA adoption of regulations identifying and listing hazardous wastes, establishing standards applicable to the generation, transportation, treatment, storage and disposal of hazardous wastes and providing for the issuance of permits authorizing the operation of hazardous waste treatment, storage, or disposal facilities.

Kentucky's General Assembly has enacted state legislation codified at KRS 224 Chapter 46 authorizing NREPC to administer the RCRA Subtitle C hazardous waste program. KRS

---

[61] Pub. L. 96-463

[62] Pub. L. 98-616

224.46-510 provides for NREPC to promulgate administrative regulations that identify and list hazardous wastes. Under the statute the state's list of hazardous waste must be "identical" to USEPA's hazardous waste list. This statutory provision has caused Kentucky's hazardous waste program to be co-extensive with the federal hazardous waste program, even though state rule-making may lag behind federal rule-making because of state statutory requirements for the promulgation of administrative regulations.

KRS 224.46-520 authorizes NREPC to regulate the treatment, storage, disposal and recycling of hazardous waste and formed the basis for the state's authorization by USEPA to administer the RCRA Subtitle C hazardous waste program that was implemented in 1980. The statute also imposes additional requirements including local government approval for certain categories of hazardous waste facilities.

KRS 224.46-530 was enacted in 1986 to provide NREPC with statutory authority to administer the HSWA Amendments that had been added to the RCRA Subtitle C hazardous waste program in 1984. Under this statute the Cabinet is authorized to impose RCRA corrective action obligations on certain permitted hazardous waste facilities, to impose minimum technological requirements on certain hazardous waste land disposal facilities, to regulate used oil and to address other regulatory issues pursuant to HSWA.

KRS Chapter Subchapter 46 includes several other provisions regarding hazardous waste for which is no federal counterpart. For example, KRS 224.46-525 directs NREPC to act on hazardous waste facility closure plans through site-specific risk-based decision making consistent with KRS 224.01-400(18) to (21) (the state's risk-based remediation statute) to the extent permissible under federal and state hazardous waste laws and regulations. Additionally, KRS

224.46-580 imposes a fee on the generation of hazardous waste the proceeds of which fund the Hazardous Waste Management Fund that is used for a number of site remediation programs.

Pursuant to Subtitle C of RCRA USEPA has promulgated administrative regulations that identify hazardous wastes and comprehensively regulate their generation, transportation, treatment, storage and disposal. The federal regulations are codified at 40 CFR Part 260 through 271. NREPC has promulgated state administrative regulations codified as 401 KAR Chapters 30 through 38 that are counterparts to the federal regulations. Some of the more significant hazardous waste regulatory provisions are outlined below.

- **40 CFR Part 261**
  401 KAR Chapter 31

These regulations identify those materials that are considered to be “solid wastes” under the federal program and which are considered to be “waste” under the state program. Federal and state terminology differ somewhat in that, under the federal program, “hazardous waste” is a sub-set of “solid waste” whereas under the state program “hazardous waste”, “solid waste’, and “special waste” are all subsets of ”waste”. In general solid waste (waste under the state program) consists of discarded material as defined in the regulation.

It is significant to note that regulatory use of the term “solid waste” does not limit the scope of the hazardous waste program to materials which are in a solid form physically since material may be a solid waste even though it is in another physical form such as liquid or sludge.

One of the most complex issues arising under the hazardous waste program involves the regulatory status of materials that are recycled or reused or are stored or treated prior to recycle or reuse. There has been a great deal of litigation involving the regulatory status of specific materials and USEPA has under consideration a number of proposals to reform its recycle-reuse regulations. The present regulatory framework is outlined in the following table:

TABLE 1				
	Use constituting disposal 401 KAR 31:010 Section 2(3)(a) (1)	**Energy recovery/fuel 401 KAR 31:010 Section 2(3)(b)(2)**	**Reclamation 401 KAR 31:010 Section 2(3)(c)(3)**	**Speculative accumulation 401 KAR 31:010 Section 2(3)(d)(4)**
Spent materials	**(waste)**	**(waste)**	**(waste)**	**(waste)**
Sludges (listed in Sections 2 or 3 of 401 KAR 31:040)	**(waste)**	**(waste)**	**(waste)**	**(waste)**
Sludges exhibiting a characteristic of hazardous waste	**(waste)**	**(waste)**	**-**	**(waste)**
By-products (listed in Sections 2 or 3 of 401 KAR 31:040)	**(waste)**	**(waste)**	**(waste)**	**(waste)**
By-products exhibiting a characteristic of hazardous waste	**(waste)**	**(waste)**	**-**	**(waste)**
Commercial chemical products listed in Section 4 of 401 KAR 31:040	**(waste)**	**(waste)**	**-**	**-**
Scrap metal	**(waste)**	**(waste)**	**(waste)**	**(waste)**

NOTE - The terms "spent materials," "sludges," "by-products," and "scrap metal" are defined in Section 1 of 401 KAR 31:005.

The regulations identify numerous categories of materials that are exempt from regulation either as a hazardous waste or as a solid waste. The exemptions include the following:

- domestic sewage and mixtures of domestic sewage and other wastes that pass through a sewer system to a publicly-owned treatment works;
- industrial wastewater discharges that are subject to regulation under the NPDES/KPDES permit program, but not the wastewater systems or sludges prior to the discharge point;
- household waste;
- certain agricultural waste returned to the soil as fertilizer;

- mining overburden returned to the mine site;
- drilling fluids, produced water and other wastes associated with hydrocarbon production;
- wastes from certain extraction, beneficiation and processing of ores and minerals;
- materials generated in product or raw material storage tanks; product or raw material transport vehicles; product or raw material pipelines or manufacturing process units until the material exits the unit in which it was generated or the unit ceases to be operated for more than 90 days;
- samples for analysis; and
- residues in empty containers as defined under the regulation.

Under 40 CFR Part 261 (401 KAR Chapter 31) a solid waste is a hazardous waste if (1) it is a category of waste that is listed (listed waste) or (2) it has the characteristic of ignitability, corrosivity, reactivity, or toxicity which are defined in the regulations (characteristic waste). Mixtures of listed hazardous waste and solid waste are regulated as a hazardous waste; however mixtures of characteristic hazardous waste and solid waste are regulated as a hazardous waste only if the resultant mixture exhibits the hazardous waste characteristic. Materials which are derived from the treatment of a listed hazardous waste are, with some exceptions, also regulated as the listed hazardous waste.

Environmental media such as soil and groundwater are not wastes; therefore, they are not subject to regulation as a hazardous waste. Nevertheless, if such environmental media have come into contact with listed hazardous wastes and contain hazardous waste constituents, the environmental media must be managed as though they were hazardous wastes unless it is established to the RCRA regulatory authority that the concentration of hazardous waste constituents is below levels that threaten human health and the environment.

Characteristic hazardous wastes are identified for regulatory purposes by the letter "D" followed by a number. For example, wastes that are hazardous by virtue of the characteristic of ignitability are identified as D001 wastes.

Listed hazardous wastes are identified by the letter "F" followed by three digits if they are from nonspecific sources such as certain spent solvents; by the letter "K" followed by three digits if they are from specific processes; and by the letter "U" or "P" followed by three digits if they are listed unused commercial chemical products, their off-specification species or spill residue of such materials.

The regulations contain special provisions that impose less stringent requirements on generators who generate or accumulate less than specified amounts of hazardous waste on a monthly basis. Such generators are referred to as conditionally exempt small quantity generators.

- **40 CFR Part 262**
  401 KAR Chapter 32

These regulations establish the standards applicable to generators of hazardous waste. The regulations also apply to persons who initiate shipments of hazardous waste from a treatment, storage, or disposal facility.

The regulations require all persons who generate waste, regardless of whether it is hazardous or not, to make a determination as to whether the waste is hazardous. The hazardous waste determination may be based upon testing of the material or may be based upon the generator's knowledge of the characteristics of the waste in light of materials or processes used.

Generators of hazardous waste are required to register with the RCRA hazardous waste regulatory agency and to obtain a USEPA identification number. Identification numbers are issued for each site at which hazardous waste is generated and generators are prohibited from managing waste or transporting it off-site prior to receiving such an identification number. In Kentucky, unlike most states, a generator who ceases generation or closes its facility must notify NREPC within 30 days of cessation of hazardous waste generation. The regulations do not require generators of hazardous waste to obtain permits unless they also conduct an activity such as treatment, storage or disposal.

Hazardous waste generators who ship hazardous waste off-site must do so under a manifest that identifies the waste and its destination. The generator must also mark containers and provide placards in accordance with U.S. Department of Transportation regulations. This regulation also establishes a procedure for hazardous waste generators to accumulate hazardous waste on-site for 90 days or less in tanks or containers without a permit or other authorization. Under the regulation such 90-day accumulators must comply with certain hazardous waste management standards and must mark the tank or container with the hazardous waste code and the date that the accumulation started. The 90-day accumulation period may be extended by the RCRA regulatory authority for an additional 30 days. Hazardous waste generators who accumulate hazardous waste on-site for longer than 90 days must obtain a hazardous waste permit. Generators who generate between 100 and 1,000 kilograms of hazardous waste per month are afforded somewhat greater flexibility under the regulations.

Under the federal regulation, generators who accumulate hazardous waste in tanks or containers under the 90-day accumulation provisions are also authorized to treat the waste in the tanks or containers without obtaining a hazardous waste permit. The state regulation has a comparable provision but imposes the additional requirement that the activity receive advance approval from the NREPC Division of Waste Management.

Hazardous waste generators may accumulate up to 55 gallons of hazardous waste in a container at or near the point of generation without complying with the requirements applicable to 90-day accumulators. Such "satellite accumulation" must take place in containers that are marked "hazardous waste".

Under the regulation hazardous waste generators are subject to reporting and recordkeeping requirements. They must also prepare and submit exception reports if the hazardous waste manifest under which hazardous waste was shipped off-site is not returned in a timely manner.

♦ **40 CFR Part 263**
401 KAR Chapter 33

These regulations establish the requirements applicable to transporters of hazardous waste. The regulations do not apply to the on-site transportation of hazardous waste by generators or on-site transportation by owners or operators of permitted hazardous waste management facilities.

Under the regulation hazardous waste transporters are required to register with NREPC and obtain an EPA identification number. Hazardous waste transporters are not required to obtain a hazardous waste permit. Additionally, hazardous waste transporters are authorized to store manifested shipments of hazardous waste at transfer facilities for up to 10 days without obtaining a permit to operate as a hazardous waste storage facility.

The principal obligation of hazardous waste transporters is to maintain the integrity of the manifest system that is critical to RCRA's cradle-to-grave hazardous waste regulatory program. The regulations also impose requirements for recordkeeping and for the removal of hazardous wastes that are released during transportation.

- **40 CFR Parts 264 and 265**
  401 KAR Chapters 34 and 35

These regulations establish the technical standards applicable to hazardous waste treatment, storage and disposal facilities. 40 CFR Part 264 and 401 KAR Chapter 34 are the federal and state standards applicable to permitted hazardous waste facilities. 40 CFR Part 265 and 401 KAR Chapter 35 are the federal and state standards applicable to hazardous waste facilities that are required to obtain a hazardous waste facility permit but have not yet received a permit. Additionally, some of the 40 CFR Part 265 (401 KAR Chapter 35) standards are incorporated by reference in 40 CFR Part 262 (401 KAR Chapter 32) as requirements for generators who accumulate and/or treat hazardous waste on-site for 90 days or less in tanks or containers and are exempt from the permit requirement.

Facilities or activities that are exempt from the technical standards include the following:

- solid waste facilities that manage only hazardous waste generated by conditionally exempt small quantity generators;
- facilities that manage certain recyclable materials;
- facilities that qualify under the 90-day accumulation provision of 40 CFR 262.34 (401 KAR 32:030);
- totally enclosed treatment facilities;
- elementary neutralization units;
- wastewater treatment units (tanks);
- immediate emergency response activities;
- transporters storing material in transit for 10 days or less;
- the combination of waste and absorbents in a container under certain circumstances; and
- handlers and transporters of universal wastes as defined in the regulations.

The hazardous waste facility standards include requirements applicable to the following activities:

- ♦ general standards regulating facilities' identification numbers, notices to other hazardous waste handlers, hazardous waste analysis, facility security, facility self-inspection, personnel training, fire prevention, and facility location in reference to seismic and flood events;
- ♦ preparedness for and prevention of hazardous waste releases including preparation and implementation of contingency plans;
- ♦ paperwork requirements such as implementation of the hazardous waste manifest system, maintenance of the facility operating records, and submission of reports;
- ♦ groundwater protection measures including monitoring and corrective action requirements;
- ♦ standards for closure of hazardous waste facilities and for postclosure care of facilities that close with waste in place;
- ♦ financial requirements including documentation of financial responsibility for closure, postclosure (if applicable) and liability;
- ♦ design and operational requirements applicable to specific types of hazardous waste facilities such as tanks, surface impoundments, waste piles, land treatment facilities, landfills, incinerators, containment buildings, miscellaneous units, and drip pads;
- ♦ air emission standards for equipment and facilities utilized in the management of hazardous wastes;
- ♦ standards for facilities used in the management of waste generated by corrective action programs.

- **40 CFR Part 266**
  401 KAR Chapter 36

These regulations establish standards and procedures applicable to certain specific hazardous wastes and hazardous waste management activities. The activities subject to this regulation include the burning of hazardous waste in boilers and industrial furnaces, the recycle of materials used for precious metal recovery, the reclamation of lead-acid batteries, the management of recyclable materials used in a manner constituting disposal such as by placement on the land surface, and management of solid waste military munitions (40 CFR Part 266 only).

- **40CFR Part 268**
  401 KAR Chapter 37

These regulations implement the hazardous waste land disposal restrictions that were added to the federal RCRA Subtitle C hazardous waste program by enactment of the HSWA Amendments of 1984 and to the Kentucky hazardous waste statute by enactment of KRS 224.46-530 in 1986. The regulations restrict the disposal of hazardous waste in surface impoundments, land treatment facilities, landfills, injection wells, waste piles and similar facilities. The regulations ban the land disposal of certain hazardous waste entirely and ban the land disposal of other hazardous wastes that have not been treated by the application of best demonstrated available technology (BDAT). The regulations exempt from the land ban provisions certain hazardous wastes including such wastes produced by small quantity generators, certain minor waste streams disposed in wastewater treatment systems and universal wastes (certain batteries, pesticides, thermostats and lighting devices).

The regulations establish BDAT for waste streams subject to land ban restrictions and prohibit the use of dilution as a substitute for treatment of the waste. The long-term storage of hazardous wastes that are subject to the land ban restrictions is also limited by the regulations.

- **40 CFR Part 270**
  401 KAR Chapter 38

These regulations establish the procedures for the issuance of permits for facilities that treat, store, or dispose of hazardous waste. The regulation contains exemptions from the permit requirement that are similar to the exemptions from applicability of the technical standards under 40 CFR Parts 264 and 265 (401 KAR Chapters 34 and 35).

Since the procedures for obtaining a hazardous waste facility permit and the consequences of regulation under such a permit can be quite onerous, the exemptions from the permit requirement play a critical role in the implementation of the RCRA Subtitle C hazardous waste program. Additionally, permits are not required of facilities that do not actively manage waste after the date that it becomes regulated under the hazardous waste program. The one-time removal of hazardous waste for purposes of disposal is not considered to be the active management of hazardous waste.

Hazardous waste management facilities that are in existence at the time they become subject to the hazardous waste permit requirements must submit an initial form called a Part A application and must comply with the interim status hazardous waste facility standards specified in 40 CFR Part 265 (401 KAR Chapter 35). Upon request of the regulatory authority administering the RCRA Subtitle C program, the owner or operator of the facility must submit a detailed permit application referred to as a Part B application. Upon issuance of the permit the facility will become subject to the hazardous waste facility standards specified in 40 CFR Part 264 (401 KAR Chapter 34). A hazardous waste facility permit must be issued prior to commencement of construction of a new hazardous waste management facility that is subject to the permit requirement.

Although the regulations identify the information that is to be included in a hazardous waste facility permit application, there is no application form that is prescribed for use. Instead the application requirements are in a narrative form. The regulations identify general information that is required of all applicants regarding the facility and its operation.

Additionally, the regulations identify specific types of facilities (such as containers or landfills) and the information that must be submitted in a permit application for that type of facility.

The Kentucky hazardous waste permit regulations include application requirements authorizing NREPC to take into account past performance in environmental compliance matters in its consideration of hazardous waste permit applications. The past performance review which is authorized under KRS 224.46-520 and implemented by administrative regulation 401 KAR 38:090 has no federal counterpart.

The regulations provide for the issuance of permits with a duration not to exceed 10 years. The permits are to include conditions necessary to achieve compliance with all requirements of the RCRA Subtitle C hazardous waste program that are applicable to the facility. Additionally, 40 CFR 270.32(b)(2) [402 KAR 38:030 Section 3(2)(b)] provides that hazardous waste facility permits are to include such conditions as are deemed necessary to protect human health and the environment. This "omnibus" provision affords the permit-issuing agency broad authority in the imposition of permit conditions.

The regulations also specify procedures to be utilized in the issuance, transfer, modification and reissuance of hazardous waste facility permits. The regulations include the following provisions:

- timetables for action on permit applications (state only);
- public participation requirements for the issuance, reissuance and major modifications of permits;
- the transfer of permits after public participation including evaluation of the past performance of the transferee;
- minor modification of permits without public participation for certain types of changes identified in the regulation; and

- the continuation in effect of expiring permits where a timely application for renewal is submitted and final administrative action has not been taken.

40 CFR Part 270 has been amended to incorporate special permit provisions implementing remedial action plans (RAP). The RAP permit procedures are intended to simplify the authorization of activities conducted in the remediation of site contamination. Many of the more burdensome aspects of the 40 CFR Part 270 hazardous waste permit program, including the requirement for site-wide corrective action, are not applicable to RAP. There is no state counterpart to the RAP procedures; however, it may be possible to utilize similar procedures under the variance provisions of administrative regulation 401 KAR 30:020 Section 2.

- **40 CFR Part 273**
  401 KAR Chapter 43

This regulation establishes management standards for so-called universal wastes. Hazardous wastes that are regulated as universal wastes under this regulation include certain spent lead-acid batteries, certain pesticides, certain thermostats and certain spent lighting devices (state only). The management standards imposed under this regulation are somewhat more lenient than those that would otherwise be applicable.

- **40 CFR Part 279**
  401 KAR Chapter 44

This regulation imposes requirements on the management of used oil. At the federal level the regulatory program is implemented under the authority of the 1980 Used Oil Recycling Act and the HSWA Amendments of 1984. At the state level the program is implemented pursuant to KRS 224.50-545 enacted in 1980 and KRS 224.46-530 enacted in 1986. The regulation applies to the generation, storage, transportation, or burning of off-specification used oil as determined by reference to criteria set forth in the regulation. The regulation does not apply to used oil generated by individuals who change their own oil, to mixtures of used oil and diesel fuel mixed on-site by used oil generators for use in their own vehicles, or to farmers who generate less than 25 gallons per month of used oil from farming equipment.

The regulation establishes standards for the following categories of used oil management:

- generators;
- collection centers and aggregation points;
- transporter and transfer facilities;
- processors and re-refiners;
- persons who burn off-specification used oil for energy recovery; and
- marketers.

The regulation also prohibits the use of used oil as a dust suppressant.

B. Non-Hazardous Waste Regulation

Subtitle D of RCRA provides for the development of federal guidelines for the disposal of non-hazardous wastes and the development of federal criteria for sanitary landfills and open dumps; however, the primary responsibility for regulation of non-hazardous wastes is allocated to state governments.

Under Kentucky law the term "waste" is used to encompass both hazardous and non-hazardous waste and the category of non-hazardous waste is divided into distinct sub-categories of solid waste and special waste.[63]

---

63 KRS 224.01-010(31)

KRS 224.01-010 defines solid waste very broadly to include garbage, refuse, sludge and other discarded materials, including solid, liquid, semi-solid or contained gaseous material resulting from industrial, commercial, mining (excluding coal mining wastes, by-products, refuse and overburden) and agricultural operations. The statute further sub-categorizes solid waste into household solid waste, commercial solid waste, industrial solid waste and municipal solid waste.

The statute excludes the following wastes from regulation under the solid waste program:

- debris extracted in state-funded construction projects;
- recovered material;
- special wastes;
- material in domestic sewage;
- manure and crop residue returned to the soil as fertilizer or soil conditioners;
- industrial point source discharges subject to the KPDES permit program; and
- material subject to regulation under the Atomic Energy Act.[64]

Solid waste, unlike hazardous waste, is not subject to a cradle-to-grave regulatory program. Instead, KRS 224.40-100 prohibits the transportation or disposal of solid waste at a site or facility that has not been issued a permit by NREPC and KRS 224.40-305 prohibits the establishment, construction, operation, maintenance or use of waste sites or facilities without the issuance of a permit by NREPC. Accordingly, the generation of solid waste is virtually unregulated, the storage and treatment of solid waste is regulated only minimally, the transportation of solid waste is regulated to insure that waste is transported to an authorized site

[64] 42 U.S.C. 2014 et seq.

or facility, and the disposal of solid waste is heavily regulated under technical standards and a comprehensive permitting system.

The most critical component of Kentucky's solid waste regulatory program is administrative regulation 401 KAR 47:030, which establishes environmental performance standards applicable to all solid waste sites and facilities. Solid waste sites and facilities that do not comply with the environmental performance standards of 401 KAR 47:030 are considered open dumps which are prohibited by state law. Kentucky's environmental performance standards are patterned after USEPA's 40 CFR Part 257 criteria for distinguishing sanitary landfills from open dumps and impose requirements in the following areas:

- flood plain protection;
- endangered species protection;
- surface water protection;
- groundwater protection;
- land application protection of food chain crops;
- polychlorinated biphenyls;
- disease protection;
- air quality protection;
- safety;
- public nuisance prevention; and
- wetland protection.

Additionally, 401 KAR 47:030 requires all waste sites and facilities to comply with all other provisions of KRS Chapter 224.

The substance of Kentucky's solid waste regulatory program is set forth in administrative regulation 401 KAR Chapter 47, which specifies the permitting requirements for solid waste sites and facilities, and in administrative regulation 401 KAR Chapter 48, which specifies the technical standards applicable to solid waste sites and facilities. Additional solid waste planning requirements are imposed in administrative regulation 401 KAR Chapter 49.

401 KAR 47:080 establishes the categories of solid waste site or facility permits, including two categories – permits-by- rule and registered permits-by-rule that impose virtually no regulatory requirements. Permits-by-rule are granted to the following categories of activities:

- most sawdust piles;
- disposal of asphalt residue;
- oil production brine pits and gas and oil drilling mud pits;
- most one-time disposal of construction material at the site of generation;
- most disposal of demolition material at the site of generation;
- on-site disposal of land clearing debris;
- limited disposal of tires;
- wastes piles;
- motor vehicle recycle and salvage yards;
- KPDES-permitted surface impoundments; and
- beneficial reuse of solid waste.

Such activities are granted a permit without submission of a permit application; however, the permit is conditioned upon compliance with the environmental performance standards of 401 KAR 47:030.

Under 401 KAR 47:080, a registered permit-by-rule is conferred upon the following activities:

- commercial recycling centers;
- transfer stations;
- construction/demolition debris landfills of one acre or less, other than at the site of generation;
- certain solid waste incinerators using refuse-derived fuels;
- sludge giveaway programs;
- certain land farming activities;
- certain septic tank pumping disposal activities; and
- convenience centers for collection and transportation of municipal solid waste.

A solid waste site or facility qualifying for a registered permit-by-rule must register with NREPC, but need not obtain an individual solid waste permit. Such site or facility must comply with the environmental performance standards of 401 KAR 47:030 and with the operational requirements of 401 KAR 47:110.

Solid waste disposal facilities subject to the permit requirement that do not qualify for a permit-by-rule or registered permit-by-rule include contained landfills, certain construction/demolition debris landfills and residual landfills. Contained landfills are authorized to accept all forms of solid waste without prior authorization from NREPC. Contained landfills must meet design and operational standards established pursuant to Subtitle D of RCRA and 401 KAR Chapter 48 and are subject to the comprehensive and time-consuming permit review procedures of KRS 224.40-310 and 401 KAR Chapter 47. Additionally, contained landfills, like all other solid waste sites or facilities, must comply with the environmental performance standards of 401 KAR 47:030.

Residual landfill is a category of solid waste landfill designed and operated to accept for disposal a limited number of industrial wastes or residues which are fully characterizable. In view of the diversity of types of industrial wastes that may be disposed in a residual landfill, 401 KAR 48:170 provides for the establishment of technical standards for residual landfills on a case-by-case basis. The case-by-case permit determinations as to the construction and design of residual landfills are to be based upon compliance with the environmental performance standards of 401 KAR 47:030.

The permit issuance procedures for solid waste landfills are set forth in KRS Chapter 224 Subchapter 40 and in 401 KAR Chapter 47. The procedures involve multiple public notice and public participation proceedings, including extensive involvement by local governing bodies. Additionally, the siting of new and expansion of existing solid waste landfills must be authorized under permit proceedings that afford aggrieved parties the opportunity to engage in trial-type administrative hearings prior to the issuance of the permit. Accordingly, whenever the siting and expansion of such facilities encounters substantial opposition, permitting of such facilities routinely involves years of administrative proceedings.

KRS 224.40-330 authorizes NREPC to consider past performance in environmental matters by applicants for solid waste site or facility permits and their key personnel. The statute allows NREPC to revoke, modify, suspend or deny a permit for a waste site or facility if it finds that an applicant or its key personnel have intentionally misrepresented or concealed material facts in the application; obtained or attempted to obtain the permit by misrepresentation or concealment; been convicted of a felony within five years preceding submission of the application; or been adjudged to have violated the federal or state environmental protection laws or regulations if NREPC determines that the violation reflects on the ability or willingness of the applicant to operate in a lawful manner. This requirement is implemented through disclosure statements prescribed by KRS 224.40-330 and 401 KRS 47:180. "Captive" facilities that accept only industrial solid waste generated by the owner/operator of the facility or its subsidiaries are exempt from the requirement to submit disclosure statements on the owner/operator and its key personnel.

In Kentucky, the universe of non-hazardous waste includes special wastes in addition to solid wastes. The Kentucky General Assembly has enacted KRS 224.50-760 directing NREPC to promulgate administrative regulations that recognize special waste as a category of non-hazardous wastes separate and distinct from the category of solid wastes. The special waste category consists of waste streams generated in large volume and posing low hazard.

Under KRS 224.50-760, special wastes consist of mining wastes, utility wastes (fly ash, bottom ash, scrubber sludge), sludge from water and wastewater treatment facilities, cement kiln dust, gas and oil drilling muds and oil production brines. In addition to the wastes specifically identified as a special waste under KRS 224.50-760, the statute also authorizes NREPC to designate additional waste streams as special wastes. NREPC has promulgated administrative regulation 401 KAR 45.210 establishing procedures for the designation of additional waste streams as special wastes, including criteria for evaluation of their status as high volume-low hazard materials.

Under Kentucky's statutes, there are several advantages that arise from classification of a waste as a special waste rather than as a solid waste. For example, the burdensome permit procedures of KRS Chapter 224 Subchapter 40, which involve multiple public notices and adversarial adjudication of siting decisons in advance of permit issuance, are inapplicable to applications for permits for disposal of special wastes. Additionally, KRS 109.041(4) precludes counties and waste management districts from regulation of special wastes, except for the land farming of water and wastewater treatment sludges and except for certain wastes from agricultural and mining operations.

NREPC has promulgated permitting and technical standards for special waste sites and facilities which are codified in 401 KAR Chapter 45. The overriding objective of these standards is to secure compliance with the environmental performance standards of 401 KAR 30:031. These environmental performance standards are similar to the environmental performance standards of 401 KAR 47:030 that apply to solid waste sites and facilities.

401 KAR 45:030 prohibits persons from engaging in the management, processing or disposal of special waste without a permit issued by NREPC. The regulation exempts from the permit requirement certain special waste management activities, including the return of certain mining wastes to the generating mine site and the management of special waste during spills and other emergency situations.

401 KAR Chapter 45 categorizes the types of special waste site or facility permits in a manner very similar to the classification of solid waste permits under 401 KAR Chapter 47. For example, special waste permits can be issued as permits-by-rule, registered permits-by-rule, emergency permits and formal permits for landfills and land farming/composting activities.

401 KAR 45:060 confers a permit-by-rule on the following activities without the necessity of a permit application:

- certain oil and gas production and brine pits;
- temporary storage of special wastes in piles;

- injection wells used for special waste disposal;
- surface mining and special waste surface impoundments;
- surface impoundments used for domestic sewage;
- disposal of coal combustion fly ash, bottom ash and scrubber sludge at certain active mining operations; and
- beneficial reuse of coal combustion by-products as an ingredient in the manufacture of products.

Each such permit-by-rule is conditioned upon compliance with the environmental performance standards of 401 KAR 30:031.

401 KAR 45:070 confers registered permit-by-rule status on sludge giveaway programs, beneficial reuse that does not qualify for a permit-by-rule, and facilities that treat and store processed sludge for composting. In order to qualify for registered permit-by-rule status, the owner/operator must register the facility with the Division of Waste Management and comply with the environmental performance standards.

Sites or facilities for the management of special waste that do not qualify for a permit-by-rule or registered permit-by-rule must be authorized under a permit issued by the Division of Waste Management under the procedures set forth in 401 KAR Chapter 45. Special waste landfills must comply with the siting requirements of 401 KAR 45:130 and with the operational requirements of other sections of 401 KAR Chapter 45. Design requirements for special waste landfills are determined on a case-by-case basis in accordance with 401 KAR 45:110.

CHAPTER 7

Underground Storage Tank Regulation

The Resource Conservation and Recovery Act ("RCRA") was amended in 1984 to regulate underground storage tanks ("USTs") which are used for the storage of petroleum products and hazardous substances. Both owners and operators of USTs are subject to the requirements of RCRA. The statutory scheme contained in Subtitle I of RCRA[65] addresses notification of the existence of USTs, design and construction requirements, reporting of releases, closure requirements and corrective action of a release. Since Kentucky has adopted by reference the majority of the Federal regulation the federal regulatory program will be discussed below.

A. Kentucky Statutory Requirements

The Kentucky statutory requirements for the regulation of USTs are contained in KRS 224.60-100 and KRS 224.60-105. NREPC is delegated the authority to regulate USTs.

B. Definitions

The scope of both the federal and state USTs programs is governed by the definition of "underground storage tank" and "regulated substances". KRS 224.60-100 and 40 CFR 280.12 define these two terms as follows:

1. "Underground storage tank" means any one (1) or combination of tanks (including underground pipes connected thereto) used to contain an accumulation

---

[65] 42 U.S.C. 6991

of regulated substances, and the volume of which (including the volume of the underground pipes connected thereto) is ten percent (10%) or more beneath the surface of the ground. Such term does not include any:

(a) Farm or residential tank of one thousand one hundred (1,100) gallons or less capacity used for storing motor fuel for noncommercial purposes;

(b) Tank used for storing heating oil for consumptive use on the premises where stored;

(c) Septic tank;

(d) Pipeline facility (including gathering lines) regulated under the Natural Gas Pipeline Safety Act of 1968, (49 U.S.C. App. 1671, et seq.), the Hazardous Liquid Pipeline Safety Act of 1979 (49 U.S.C. App. 2001 et seq.), or which is an intrastate pipeline facility regulated under state laws comparable to the provisions of the Natural Gas Pipeline Safety Act of 1968 or the Hazardous Liquid Pipeline Safety Act of 1979;

(e) Surface impoundment pit, pond, or lagoon;

(f) Storm water or waste water collection system;

(g) Flow-through process tank;

(h) Liquid trap or associated gathering lines directly related to oil or gas production and gathering operations; or

(i) Storage tank situated in an underground area (such as a basement, cellar, mineworking, drift, shaft, or tunnel) if the storage tank is situated upon or above the surface of a floor.

2. "Regulated substance" means any substance defined in Section 101(14) of the Comprehensive Environmental Response, Compensation, and Liability Act of 1980, but not including any substance regulated as a hazardous waste under Subtitle C, and petroleum, including crude oil or any fraction thereof which is liquid at standard conditions of temperature and pressure (60 degrees Fahrenheit and 14.7 pounds per square inch absolute).

C. Specific UST System Exclusions

Specific UST systems which are excluded from regulation under the Kentucky program are identified in 401 KAR 42.011(1). Specifically excluded are:

- UST systems containing wastes identified as hazardous in 401 KAR Chapter 31, and UST systems containing mixtures of hazardous waste and other regulated substances;

- Wastewater treatment tank systems that are part of a wastewater treatment facility regulated under the Clean Water Act, as amended (33 USC 1251 et seq.);

- Equipment and machinery containing regulated substances for operational purposes, such as hydraulic lift tanks and electrical equipment tanks;

- UST systems having a capacity of 110 gallons or less;

- UST systems containing a de minimis concentration of regulated substances;

- Emergency spill or overflow containment UST systems that are emptied immediately after use; and

- UST systems excluded from the definition of"underground storage tank" provided in KRS 224.60-100.

D. Deferrals

Certain specific UST systems which are deferred from compliance with requirements of 401 KAR Chapter 42 are:

- 401 KAR 42:040 does not apply to UST systems that store fuel solely for use by emergency power generators.

- 401 KAR 42:020, 401 KAR 42:030, 401 KAR 42:040, and 401 KAR 42:050 do not apply to the following UST systems:

    - ♦ Wastewater treatment tank systems that are not part of a wastewater treatment facility regulated under the Clean Water Act, as amended (33 USC 1251 et seq.);

    - ♦ UST systems containing radioactive material that are regulated under the Atomic Energy Act of 1954, as amended (42 USC 2011 et seq.);

    - ♦ UST systems that are part of an emergency generator system at a nuclear power generation facility regulated by the Nuclear Regulatory Commission under Appendix A of 10 C.F.R Part 50;

- Airport hydrant fuel distribution systems; and
- UST systems with field-constructed tanks.

E. Notification Requirements

Kentucky has adopted by reference at 401 KAR 42:020 the federal requirements for notification contained in 40 CFR 280.22. The federal provisions provide that any owner who brings an underground storage tank system into use after May 8, 1986 must, within 30 days of bringing such tank into use, notify the designated state or local agency or department.

Owners and operators of UST systems that were in the ground on or after May 8, 1986, unless taken out of operation on or before January 1, 1974, were required to notify the designated state or local agency in accordance with the Hazardous and Solid Waste Amendments of 1984 (HSWA) unless notice was given pursuant to Section 103(c) of CERCLA.[66]

NREPC in 401 KAR 42:200 Section 3 requires amended notification within 30 days of any changes to ownership of the UST system, description of the UST system or financial responsibility. If an unregistered UST system is discovered during permanent closure activities, an amended notification must be submitted to NREPC.

F. Design and Construction Requirements

Kentucky adopted by reference in 401 KAR 42:020, the federal requirements for design, construction and installation contained in 40 CFR 280.20. In order to prevent releases

[66] 42 U.S.C. 9603

due to structural failure, corrosion, or spills and overfills, new systems must meet the following requirements:

- Tanks must be properly designed and constructed and any portion underground that routinely contains product must be protected from corrosion as follows:
  - ♦ The tank must be constructed of fiberglass-reinforced plastic;
  - ♦ If the tank is constructed of steel it must be cathodically protected;
  - ♦ The tank must be constructed of a steel fiberglass-reinforced plastic composite; or
  - ♦ If the tank is constructed of metal without additional corrosion protection measures it will be allowed if a corrosion expert determines that it is not corrosive enough to cause it to have a release due to corrosion.
- Piping that routinely contains regulated substances and is in contact with the ground must be properly designed, constructed, and protected from corrosion. The same criteria for materials as set forth above for tanks apply to piping.
- Spilled overfill prevention equipment. In order to prevent spilling and overfilling associated with product transfer to the UST system, spill and overfill prevention equipment including catchment basins, automatic shut off valves when the tank is 95% full, alarms or restricted flow devices which alert the operator when the tank is no more than 90% full.
- Installation. All tanks and piping must be properly installed in accordance with a code of practice developed by a nationally recognized association or independent testing laboratory and in accordance with the manufacturer's instructions.
- Certification of installation. All owners and operators must ensure that the installer has been certified by the tank and piping manufacturer, the implementing agency, or the installation has been inspected and certified by a registered professional engineer with education and experience in UST systems.
- Upgrading of existing UST systems. No later than December 22, 1998, all existing UST systems must comply with one of the following requirements:
  - ♦ New UST system performance standards.
  - ♦ Upgraded including the use of interior lining, cathodic protection, piping upgrading and spill and overfill prevention equipment.

- Closure of the tank and any necessary remedial corrective action requirements in accordance with 40 CFR 280.7-74.

G. General Operating Requirements

Owners and operators must ensure that releases due to spilling or overfilling do not occur. The owner and operator must report, investigate, and clean up any spills and overfills in accordance with 40 CFR 280.53. All owners and operators of steel UST systems with corrosion protection must be operated and maintained to continuously provide corrosion protection. All UST systems equipped with cathodic protection systems must be inspected for proper operation by a qualified cathodic protection tester with a specific frequency. Owners and operators must use a UST system made of or lined with materials that are compatible with the substance stored in the UST system.

Owners and operators must ensure that repairs will prevent releases due to structural failure or corrosion. Owners and operators must fully cooperate with inspections, monitoring and testing conducted by the agency, and all record keeping report requirements.

H. Release Detection

NREPC has adopted by reference in 401 KAR 42:040 the federal regulatory requirements for Release Reporting contained in 40 CFR 280.40.

Owners and operators of new and existing UST systems must provide a method of release detection that can detect a release from any portion of the tank and connected underground piping; be installed, calibrated, operated and maintained in accordance with the manufacturer's instructions; and meet the performance requirements of 40 CFR 280.43 or 40 CFR 280.44. When a release detection method operated in accordance with the performance standards indicates a release may have occurred, owners and operators must notify the implementing agency. Any existing UST system that cannot apply a method of release detection that complies with the regulations must complete closure.

Owners and operators of petroleum UST systems must provide release detection for tanks and piping. Tanks must be monitored at least every 30 days for releases using the methods specified in 40 CFR 280.43 unless specific standards are met. Piping also has specific monitoring for release standards.

Owners and operators of UST systems for hazardous substances must provide release detection based upon whether the UST system is new or existing. New hazardous substance UST systems must have secondary containment systems, double-walled tanks, and external liners. Underground piping must also be equipped with secondary containment.

Release detection methods for tanks must consist of inventory control, manual tank gauging, tank tightness testing, automatic tank gauging, vapor monitoring, groundwater monitoring and interstitial monitoring.

I. Release Reporting, Investigation and Confirmation

Owners and operators must report releases or suspected releases to the state agency within twenty-four (24) hours, unless a different time period is specified. Owners and operators must immediately investigate and confirm all suspected releases of regulated substances within 7 days unless otherwise specified. Owners must perform system test (tightness testing in 40 CFR 280.43 and 40 CFR 280.44) to determine whether a leak exists in the tank. Owners must repair, replace or upgrade UST systems and begin corrective action as required in 40 CFR 280.60 if the systems test, tank or delivery piping indicates that a leak exists. Further investigation is not necessary if the test results for the system, tank and delivery piping do not indicate that a leak exists and if environmental contamination is not the basis for suspecting a release.

Owners and operators must contain and immediately clean up a spill or overfill and notify the implementing agency within 24 hours or other time period specified by the agency. Unless directed otherwise, operators must remove as much of the regulated substances from the UST system as is necessary to prevent further releases.

Operators must, within 45 days of the release, submit initial site characterizations to the agency. Where an investigation indicates the presence of free product, the free product must be removed to the extent practicable. In order to determine the full extent and location of soils contaminated by the release and the presence and concentration of dissolved product contamination in the groundwater, owners and operators must conduct investigation of the release, release site and surrounding area if any of the following conditions exist: (a) evidence that groundwater wells are affected, (b) free product is required to be recovered, (c) there is evidence that contaminated soils may be in contact with groundwater, (d) the agency requests an investigation.

J. Release Response and Corrective Action

A corrective action plan for responding to contaminated soil or groundwater shall be submitted to the agency within the time period specified by the agency. Upon approval of the corrective action plan, the plan must be implemented.

For each release that requires a corrective action plan, the agency must provide notice to the public. Before approving a corrective action plan, the agency may hold a public hearing.

K. Active Service, Temporary and Permanent Closure of UST Systems

If a UST system is temporarily closed, operation and maintenance of corrosion protection must continue and release detection must be maintained unless the system is empty. A UST system is empty if no more than 1 inch of residue, or .3% by weight of the total capacity of the UST system, remains in the system. Additional requirements must be met if the UST system is closed for 3 months or more.

At least 30 days before beginning permanent closure, the agency must be notified of such intended closure. To permanently close a tank it must be emptied and cleaned by removing all liquids and sludges. The tank must be removed from the ground or filled with an inert solid material. Additionally, before final closure the presence of a release must be measured where contamination is most likely to be present. Closure records must be maintained for at least 3 years after completion of permanent closure.

L. Out of Service UST Systems and Closure

When a UST system is temporarily closed, owners and operators must continue operation and maintenance of corrosion protection and any release detection requirements unless the UST system is empty. Empty is defined as when all materials have been removed using commonly employed practices so that no more than 2.5 centimeters (one inch) of residue, or 0.3 percent by weight of the total capacity of the system, remains in the system. Additional measures must be employed based upon the duration of the temporary closure with three months and twelve months being the time periods for increased protection measures.

At least 30 days prior to permanent closure or change in service the owner and operator must notify the implementing agency and before permanent closure must measure for the presence of a release where contamination is most likely to be present. If contaminated soils, contaminated groundwater or free product is discovered then the owner and operator shall begin corrective action.

When directed by the implementing agency, the owner and operator of a UST system permanently closed before December 22, 1998 must assess the excavation zone and close the UST system in accordance with current requirements. Closure records that are capable of demonstrating compliance with applicable closure requirements shall be maintained for at least 3 years after completion of the closure.

M. Financial Responsibility

Financial responsibility is the obligation of either the owner or the operator; both parties are not required to demonstrate financial responsibility. However, both parties are liable in the event of a non-compliance.

Owners or operators of petroleum USTs must demonstrate financial responsibility for taking corrective action and for compensating third parties for bodily injury and property damage caused by accidental releases. For petroleum storage tanks located at petroleum marketing facilities or that handle an average of 10,000 gallons of petroleum per month, $1,000,000 coverage is required. For all other owners or operators of USTs, $400,000 coverage is required. These amounts are per occurrence. The aggregate amount of coverage required for owners or operators of 1 to 100 petroleum UST is $1,000,000 and for owners or operators of 101 or more USTs, $2,000,000.

Owners or operators may demonstrate financial responsibility by self insurance, by guarantee, insurance coverage, letter of credit, or surety bond.

N. Kentucky Petroleum Storage Tank Environmental Assurance Fund

Each participating petroleum UST owner or operator is required to establish and maintain evidence of financial responsibility for taking corrective action and for compensating third parties for bodily injury and property damage. The amount of financial responsibility is on a sliding scale based upon the number of tanks owned or operated.

For owners or operators with eleven or more tanks the level of financial responsibility to be established and maintained is $12,500 dollars per occurrence for taking corrective action and $12,500 per occurrence for compensating third parties for bodily injury and property damage. The required amount of financial responsibility decreases based upon the fewer tanks owned or operated. When the Kentucky General Assembly enacted KRS 224.60-140, it intended that the fund established by that enactment could be used by owners and operators to demonstrate their compliance with requirements for financial responsibility.

The money contained in the Fund established by KRS 224.60-140 may be used to reimburse petroleum UST owners or operators for the costs and expenses incurred for corrective action or for the payment of or reimbursement for third party claims for bodily injury and property damage. The use of the fund can not exceed $1,000,000 per occurrence for corrective action and $1,000,000 per occurrence for compensating third parties.

To be eligible to participate in the fund, the owner of any petroleum UST containing motor fuels currently existing or removed after January 1, 1974 must register the tanks with the Cabinet prior to applying to the fund.

KRS 224.60-120(6) establishes a financial responsibility account which may be used by petroleum UST owners and operators to demonstrate financial responsibility. Owner and operators must meet certain requirements to be eligible to participate in the account. These include registration of tanks, having release detection, corrosion protection and paid annual dues.

CHAPTER 8

Environmental Regulation of Mining

A. Introduction

Unlike the other programs covered in this book, environmental aspects of mining are not regulated primarily by the Department for Environmental Protection but by the Department for Surface Mining, Reclamation and Enforcement ("DSMRE"), a department within NREPC. Although the Department for Environmental Protection exercises some minimal authority over mining operations in Kentucky, the primary mining enforcement arm of NREPC is DSMRE. DSMRE's permit review staff is located in Frankfort, while DSMRE's enforcement/inspection staff is located both in Frankfort and in five regional offices. The entire Department is headed by a commissioner and several directors, all of whom are appointed by the Governor. Health and safety impacts of surface coal mining to the public are regulated by DSMRE pursuant to KRS Chapter 350. However, health and safety impacts of coal mining on miners is regulated at the federal level by the Mine Safety and Health Administration ("MSHA"), U.S. Department of Labor, and at the state level by the Kentucky Department of Mines and Minerals which is in the Public Protection and Regulation Cabinet. This Chapter does not address regulation of health and safety aspects of coal mining as regulated by MSHA or the Kentucky Department of Mines and Minerals.

Kentucky's surface coal mining program achieved "primacy" from the federal Office of Surface Mining, Reclamation Enforcement ("OSM") in 1982 following the enactment by Congress in August of 1977 of the Surface Mining Control and Reclamation Act of 1977

("SMCRA")[67]. SMCRA established new permitting and enforcement requirements, and required each state to adopt a state regulatory program at least as stringent as the federal program. Kentucky was given by OSM the primary responsibility for regulating mining in May of 1982. The majority of Kentucky's mining regulatory program is set forth in KRS Chapter 350 and in 405 KAR Chapter 7 through Chapter 24. In addition to this statute and these regulations, the Cabinet also has jurisdiction over surface mining through its general authority set forth at KRS Chapter 224. The Cabinet has further authority over mining by virtue of KRS Chapter 151 (Geology and Water Resources).

B. Kentucky's Environment Regulation of Coal Mining - An Outline

(1) Permits

The permit is the heart of the environmental regulation of coal mining. It enables the regulatory authority to prescribe the terms and conditions for mining generally and is tailored to the particular site to be mined. The permit serves two functions: (1) to require the mine operator to plan the operation in detail and to identify and avoid adverse environmental impacts and to facilitate site reclamation; and (2) to provide the regulatory authority broad inspection and enforcement powers over the mining operation.

The Kentucky regulations setting forth permit requirements for conducting surface coal mining and reclamation operations are found in 405 KAR Chapter 8. These regulations specify when permits are required, application deadlines, technical permit requirements, fees, review procedures, public notice requirements, informal and formal submission of public comments on permit applications, criteria for permit approval or denial and relevant actions, terms and

[67] 30 U.S.C. 1201 et seq.

conditions of permits, review of outstanding (existing) permits, revision of permits, amendments and renewals, transfers, assignments, and sales of permit rights, administrative and judicial review procedures, and procedures relating to improvidently-issued permits.

The review of permit applications begins with a DSMRE determination of whether the application is complete. The DSMRE then determines whether the applicant is currently in violation of any federal or state surface mining regulation or other programmatic requirements pertaining to environmental protection.

The time frame in which DSMRE permit approval or denial actions must be taken is contained in 405 KAR 8:010 Section16. Permits are generally issued for a term not to exceed five years, although a longer permit term may be granted at the discretion of the DSMRE.

One who accepts a permit issued by the DSMRE, or begins operations pursuant to such a permit, is deemed to have knowledge of the conditions set forth in the applicable regulations and to have accepted them, whether or not such conditions are set forth in the specific permit. In general, these conditions require that a permittee comply fully with all terms and conditions of the permit and conduct surface coal mining and reclamation operations only on those lands specifically designated on the map or maps submitted with the permit application. Also, the permittee is subject to the regulatory right of entry upon the permit area. Finally, the permittee must agree to take all possible steps to minimize any adverse impact to the environment or to the public health and safety resulting from failure to comply with any term or condition of the permit.

405 KAR 8:010 also sets forth procedures for DSMRE review of outstanding permits, revisions to existing permits, permit renewals for permit areas covered under the current permit, and amending permits in order to add a new area to the existing permit area. The regulation also

requires the written approval of NREPC for any transfer, assignment or sale of the rights granted under any permit issued under 405 KAR Chapter 8.

Finally, this regulation prescribes procedures for administrative and judicial review, and authorizes the DSMRE to take certain remedial steps if it has improvidently issued a permit. If the DSMRE determines that, because of an unabated violation or a delinquent penalty or fee, it improvidently issued a permit, it may (a) implement a plan for abatement or payment; (b) impose on the permit a condition requiring the responsible party to abate the violation or pay the fee; (c) suspend the permit until payment or abatement; or (d) rescind the permit.

(a) The Permit as an Enforcement Tool - The Permit Block

The permit block is one of the most powerful enforcement tools available to regulatory authorities. Section 510(c)[68] of SMCRA and the comparable Kentucky law[69] prohibits operators with current violations or histories of wilful violations from obtaining additional permits. Any applicant for a surface mining permit must file with the permit application a listing of notices of noncompliances of KRS Chapter 350, and of any law, rule, or regulation pertaining to air or water environmental protection, incurred in connection with any surface coal mining operation during the previous three years. Mandatory denial of a permit occurs in two instances:

(i) Where the schedule or other information available to DSMRE indicates that any surface coal mining operation owned or controlled by the applicant is currently in violation, the permit shall not be issued until the applicant submits proof that such violation has been corrected

---

68 30 U.S.C. 1260(c)

69 KRS 350.130

or is in the process of being corrected to the satisfaction of the regulatory authority, which has jurisdiction over such violation; and

(ii) No permit shall be issued to an applicant after a finding by the regulatory authority, after opportunity for hearing, that the applicant, or the operator specified in the application, controls or has controlled mining operations with a demonstrated pattern of wilful violations of such nature and duration with such resulting irreparable damage to the environment as to indicate an intent not to comply with the provisions of KRS Chapter 350.

The permit block provisions of SMCRA are intended:

- to deter violations and the failure to reclaim,
- to secure correction of violations by blocking permit issuance to anyone with current or outstanding violations, and
- to permanently bar "bad actors" from mining.

The permit block is a very effective enforcement and compliance tool because it creates an ability to deny permission to mine. The permit block provision places the burden of demonstrating current compliance on the applicant. The permit block is particularly useful to states wishing to secure correction of a violation by a large operator that may have applications pending in other states. The applicant has a strong economic incentive to avoid delays in the approval of a permit application. Thus, the permit block provides an impetus for early abatement of violations when a permit application is pending. Finally, the permit block is the single strongest disincentive to abandonment of an unreclaimed site, since it can bar an operator from ever operating again.

The permit block system is designed to find any links between a permit applicant and owners or operators with violations. These links may cross state lines, because many coal companies operate in several states.

(b) Permit Block Implementation

Each state regulatory authority including DSMRE is responsible for withholding permits if SMCRA's blocking criteria are met. OSM is responsible for permit blocking in states that do not have primacy and for oversight of state permit blocking. Additionally, because the system must operate across state lines - using, for example, Kentucky violations to block Virginia permit applications, OSM has attempted to coordinate interstate transfer of data by establishing a computerized information system, the Applicant Violator System ("AVS").

(c) The AVS

The federal AVS was developed under a court order requiring the Secretary of the Interior to establish a computerized system to match permit applicants and their owners or controllers with SMCRA violators. In 1986, Congress directed OSM to expand the system to include information on unpaid abandoned mine land fees and information on unabated state cessation orders ("COs"), unpaid state civil penalties, and other federal and state air or water violations tied to surface mining.

The AVS contains violation and ownership and control data. Permit application information is entered into the AVS by the state regulatory agency. The permit request is then sent to the main AVS which can verify information. The computer can link entities using information such as name, address, Social Security number, the Mine Safety and Health Administration ("MSHA") I.D. number, or permit number.

(2) Bonding Requirements

DSMRE must require a posting of a reclamation bond in an amount sufficient to assure that the commitments set forth in the permit are carried out. 405 KAR Chapter 10 contains the specific requirements regarding bonding methods and minimum requirements. Bonds must be filed with DSMRE once a permit has been approved for issuance. Bond amounts are determined in accordance with the provisions of 405 KAR 10:020. A bond is to be set in an amount adequate to allow DSMRE to reclaim the mine site if the operator is unable or unwilling to fulfill its obligations. Liability under the bond lasts for the life of the surface mining and reclamation operation and for as long thereafter as the operator remains responsible for establishing successful revegetation. If the operator successfully completes the required reclamation, the bond is released.

Bonds are subject to forfeiture for failure to timely and/or satisfactorily complete reclamation or for other noncompliances with regulatory requirements. Once a bond has been forfeited, neither the permittee nor persons/entities that own or control the permittee nor persons/entities who the permittee owns or controls may obtain a new permit in any state until the property has been fully reclaimed and/or the violation in question is fully abated.

Bonds are generally released in phases and the procedures and criteria for such release or partial release of bonds are contained in 405 KAR 10:050. This regulation also sets forth the various types, terms and conditions that DSMRE will accept in satisfaction of the bonding requirement, including surety bonds, letters of credit and certificates of deposit.

(3) Inspection and Enforcement

The inspection and enforcement provisions contained in KRS Chapter 350 and 405 KAR Chapter 12 are adopted in large part from the inspection and enforcement provisions of SMCRA and OSM's enforcement and inspection regulations promulgated pursuant to SMCRA. This is because of the federal requirement contained in SMCRA that all state programs, including the enforcement provisions thereof, must be as effective as the federal provisions.

405 KAR Chapter 12 directs that inspections be made at irregular intervals without prior notice to the permittee or operator. This Chapter also sets forth provisions concerning inspection frequencies as well as the rights of the public to participate in the enforcement process. KRS Chapter 12 also contains specific civil and criminal penalty provisions.

DSMRE must conduct a partial inspection of a surface coal mining and reclamation operations at least monthly for each area affected until phase I (grading and seeding) reclamation has been completed on the entire permit area. These partial inspections must be continued until DSMRE determines that the permit area is sufficiently stable so that quarterly inspections will provide adequate inspection of the permit area. DSMRE must conduct an average of at least one complete inspection per calendar quarter of each area affected by mining and reclamation activities.

405 KAR 12:020 provides for the issuance of notices of noncompliance and orders for remedial measures in the event of a violation. Additionally, an order for cessation and immediate compliance will be issued for failure to abate a violation within the specified abatement period. A cessation order shall also be issued when the inspector believes that an imminent danger or a significant, imminent environmental harm exists regardless of a whether a violation exists. Procedures are also prescribed for the suspension or revocation of a permit in the event that a pattern of violations is established.

In accordance with 405 KAR 12:030, persons who have an interest which is, or may be, adversely affected by the issuance, modification, vacation, or termination of a notice or order regarding inspection or enforcement may participate at every significant level of the administrative process. The requirements and procedures for such public participation are set out more specifically in 405 KAR 12:030.

(4) Federal Oversight and Enforcement

Although DSMRE has primary regulatory authority in all matters regarding environmental regulation of coal mining, OSM has oversight authority under SMCRA in enforcement matters in particular cases. The rights of OSM to take federal enforcement in a state with an improved state program are spelled out in 30 CFR Parts 842 (Federal Inspections and Monitoring) and 843 (Federal Enforcement). Essentially, if OSM has reason to believe on the basis of information available to it (from a citizen's complaint or otherwise) that a violation of SMCRA or of state law exists or that there exists an imminent danger to the health or safety of the public or that there exists or that it could reasonably be expected to exist a significant, imminent environmental harm to land, air or water resources, OSM may take enforcement action under the federal SMCRA enforcement procedures specified in 30 CFR Part 843. Such action may be taken if OSM has notified DSMRE of the possible violation, more than 10 days have elapsed since notification and DSMRE has failed to take "appropriate" action to cause the violation to be corrected or to show cause to OSM for such failure. OSM is not required to wait for DSMRE "appropriate action" in cases of imminent danger or "significant imminent environmental harm."

After receiving a response from DSMRE, and before conducting a federal inspection, OSM must determine in writing whether the standards for "appropriate action" or for "good cause" for such failure have been meet. If OSM believes that the above-referenced standards have not been met by DSMRE, it may proceed to take appropriate federal enforcement action unless barred by legal action brought by the permittee or operator. Much litigation has been brought by coal operators over this federal-state overlap in the area of inspection and enforcement of surface coal mining and reclamation operations.

Federal inspections may be requested by any person who makes a signed, written statement that would lead OSM to believe that a violation and/or imminent danger exists and that DSMRE has been notified of such violation or practice.

(5) Performance Standards for Mining and Reclamation Activities

405 KAR Chapter 16 sets forth the performance standards for the protection of land, water, natural resources and aesthetic values during the course of surface coal mining and reclamation activities. Included within its purview are specific standards relating to contemporaneous reclamation, signs and markers, topsoil, hydrology, water quality standards and effluent limitations, design and construction of temporary diversions, sedimentation ponds, permanent and temporary impoundments, surface and ground water monitoring, use of explosives, disposal of excess spoil, disposal of coal processing waste, coal processing waste dams and impoundments, protection of fish and wildlife, backfilling and grading, revegetation, postmining land use, roads and other "facilities."

Performance standards, which are set forth in 405 KAR Chapter 18, were promulgated for the protection of land, water and other natural resources of those surface areas that are affected by underground mining activities. To a great extent, these performance standards mirror many of the standards that are set forth under the performance standards for surface coal mining and reclamation activities.

Special performance standards are contained in 405 KAR 20:010 through 405 KAR 20:080. These special performance standards deal with the following topics: coal exploration, auger mining, prime farm land, mountaintop removal, steep slope mining, off site coal processing plants, and in situ processing.

(6) Lands Unsuitable for Mining

405 KAR 24:020 through 405 KAR 24:040 deals with the process by which DSMRE determines whether proposed surface coal mining and reclamation operations either are subject to limitations and prohibitions enacted by Congress or the Kentucky General Assembly, or whether other such areas may be deemed unsuitable for all or certain types of surface coal mining operations, through the petition process.

405 KAR 24:020 and 405 KAR 24:030 deal with the minimum requirements that petitioners must meet when seeking the designation of certain lands as unsuitable for all or certain types of surface coal mining operations as well as the procedures and criteria for DSMRE review of such petitions. 405 KAR 24:040 deals with DSMRE review of permit applications to determine whether or not the proposed operations would be subject to limitations or prohibitions contained in federal or state surface mining statutes. Specifically 405 KAR 24:040 Section 2 sets forth seven discrete areas as being unsuitable for mining unless the operations existed on August 3, 1977, or unless required approvals or waivers have been obtained subject to "valid existing rights." The seven areas are as follows: (1) Lands within boundaries of the National Park System, the National Wildlife Refuge System, the National Systems of Trails, the National Wilderness Preservation System, the Wild and Scenic River System, and National Recreation Areas; (2) Lands within 300 feet of any public park, public building, school, church or community or institutional building; (3) Lands within 100 feet of a cemetery; (4) Lands which will adversely affect any publicly-owned park or publicly-owned place included on the National Register of Historic Places; (5) Lands within 300 feet of any occupied dwelling (unless the

owner of the dwelling has provided a written waiver consenting to mining closer than 300 feet); (6) Lands within100 feet of the right-of-way line of any public road; and (7) Federal lands within the boundaries of any National Forest unless approved by the Secretary of the Interior.

(7) Hearing and Appeals Process

405 KAR 7:091, together with 405 KAR 7:092, sets forth provisions dealing with hearings, penalty assessment, notice and other procedural provisions relating to administrative review of enforcement actions taken by DSMRE.

(8) Rulemaking Petitions

DSMRE is required by statute[70] to have a procedure in its surface mining regulatory program for persons to petition the Secretary of the Cabinet to initiate a rulemaking process to develop new regulations or to modify existing regulations. 405 KAR 7:110 specifies how one may initiate this process, including the contents of a petition, time limits for review of such petitions and other procedural aspects of the process.

C. Environmental Regulation of Non-Coal Mining

(1) Permitting

A permit is required from NREPC prior to the mining of non-coal minerals, including the mining of limestone and dolomite; mining of sand and gravel, surface disturbance of dredging of river or creek sand and gravel; mining of clay; mining of fluorspar and other vein minerals. "Mineral operations" includes the surface disturbance of underground mining as well as surface mining. The specific requirements for obtaining permits for such operations are

[70] KRS 350.255

contained in 405 KAR 5:030. No person engaging in such operations is allowed to throw, pile, dump or otherwise dispose of any overburden, stones, shale, dirt, debris, trees or other substance outside the area designated as the permit area. In addition, no person may engage in any practice which constitutes an imminent danger to the health or safety of the public or that would be likely to cause a significant, imminent environmental harm to land, air or water resources.

(2) Performance Standards

405 KAR 5:035 through 5:070 contain the performance standards which NREPC has established for non-coal mining operations to meet. These standards include provisions dealing with signs and markers, blasting, access roads and haul roads, protection of environmental resources, protection of surface water quantity and quality, impoundments, handling of materials, premining and postmining land use and revegetation.

(3) Bonding

405 KAR 5:080 relates to bonding of non-coal mining operations. Essentially, no reclamation bond is required unless NREPC finds that the operation is to be temporary or that the permit applicant has an unacceptable mining record in Kentucky.

(4) Enforcement

405 KAR 5:085 contains the enforcement provisions relating to regulation of non-coal mining. Inspection personnel of DSMRE are deemed authorized representatives of NREPC for purposes of inspection and enforcement. Inspections are made randomly with no prescribed number of inspections being established. Inspectors are authorized to issue notices of noncompliance and order for remedial measures as well as cessation orders, much like the enforcement powers prescribed for the regulation of coal mining.

(5) Hearings and Informal Settlement Conferences

405 KAR 5:095 deals with the rights of non-coal mineral operators to administratively challenge or informally confer with NREPC in connection with any order or determination made by NREPC in connection with the regulation of non-coal mineral operators.

(6) Oil Shale Operations

Oil shale operations are regulated by NREPC under a separate portion of the regulations, specifically 405 KAR Chapter 30. That chapter contains provisions relating to such areas as experimental practices, performance bonds, inspection and enforcement, oil shale performance standards, operation permits and insurance requirements.

CHAPTER 9

Release Reporting and Remediation in Kentucky

Since the enactment of the Comprehensive Environmental Response Compensation and Liability Act, (CERCLA) in 1980[71], the requirements for notification and remediation of releases to the environment have been a major aspect of environmental law. In Kentucky, as in other states, CERCLA and other media-specific federal requirements establish the baseline for release notification and remediation. Kentucky has, however, established a state release notification and remediation program that serves as the primary regulatory program applicable to most instances of releases and environmental contamination in the state.

A. Release Reporting

Release reporting in Kentucky reflects a combination of federal and state requirements. At the federal level CERCLA Section 103[72] provides that the person in charge of a vessel or facility must, upon obtaining knowledge of a release into the environment of a hazardous substance in a reportable quantity, notify the National Response Center. The reporting obligation does not apply to federally permitted releases or to releases of petroleum since petroleum is not included within the statutory definition of hazardous substance.

---

71 42 U.S.C. 9601 et seq.

72 42 U.S.C. 9603

The terms "release" and "facility" are very broadly defined in CERCLA Section 101[73]. Additionally, the meaning of the term "environment" is important to the CERCLA release reporting requirement since only releases into the "environment" are subject to the reporting requirement. CERCLA Section 101 defines "environment" as including all surface water, groundwater, land surface or subsurface strata or ambient air within the United States. The term does not include buildings or other impervious engineered structures such as concrete dikes. Accordingly, material released from a storage tank into an impervious diked area would not be included in determining whether the release was in a reportable quantity; however, any amount of the material that volatilized from the diked area into the atmosphere would be included.

The release reporting requirement of CERCLA Section 103 is implemented by regulations codified at 40 CFR Part 302. These regulations establish a list of hazardous substances and the reportable quantity for each substance. The regulations provide that the reportable quantity shall be determined on the basis of releases occurring within a 24-hour timeframe.

The release of mixtures of hazardous substances raises a number of issues as to the reporting requirement. Under 40 CFR Part 302, if the concentration of each individual substance in the mixture is known, the reportable quantity for each hazardous substance is compared with the amount of the specific hazardous substance that was released, in order to determine whether the release was in a reportable quantity. On the other hand, if the concentration of specific hazardous substances in the mixture is unknown, the entire amount of the mixture is compared

---

[73] 42 U.S.C. 9601

with the reportable quantity for the hazardous substance in the mixture that has the lowest reportable quantity in order to determine whether the reporting requirement was triggered.

CERCLA Section 103 has specific provisions relating to the reporting of continuous releases of hazardous substances to the environment. If such releases are stable in quantity and rate, the person in charge of the vessel or facility may be afforded the opportunity to avoid repeated notification of the releases.

"Federally permitted releases" are exempt from the release reporting requirement of CERCLA Section 103. The scope of the exemption has been a source of confusion since the enactment of the statute. The exemption is intended to obviate the necessity to notify the National Response Center of those releases that have been specifically authorized under environmental protection programs such as the Clean Water Act NPDES/KPDES permit program and similar federal regulatory programs. The theory of the exemption is that the purpose of the notification, to allow federal agencies to determine whether to undertake response or remediation activities, was satisfied when the permit authorizing the release was issued. The major areas of controversy have involved issues such as whether a permit authorizing the emission of specific amounts of a volatile organic compound should be viewed as authorizing the release of the same amounts of each hazardous substance that is a component of the compound. Similar issues have been raised as to whether emission regulations that specify threshold amounts below which emissions are not subject to regulation should be construed as authorizing the release of specific substances in amounts below the regulatory threshold but in amounts above the CERCLA reportable quantity without notification of the National Response Center. EPA has issued guidance documents in an effort to clarify the scope of the "federally permitted release" exemption from CERCLA release notification.

Another major federal release reporting program was established by the enactment in 1986 of the Environmental Planning and Community Right-to-Know Act (EPCRA also known as SARA Title III)[74]. Section 304 of EPCRA[75] requires the owner or operator of a facility from which there has been a release of a hazardous substance or an extremely hazardous substance in a reportable quantity to notify the local emergency planning committee for all areas likely to be affected by the release and the state emergency response committee of all states likely to be affected by the release. No notification is required under EPCRA if the only exposure from the release is to persons within the facility.

EPCRA Section 304 has been implemented by the promulgation of administrative regulations codified at 40 CFR Part 355. The regulations identify extremely hazardous substances and their reportable quantities. The release notification requirements under EPCRA Section 304 are comparable in many respects to the release reporting requirements under CERCLA Section 103. For example reportable quantities for mixtures are calculated similarly, reportable quantities are determined on a 24-hour basis, federally permitted releases are exempt from notification and continuous releases are subject to special notification procedures.

The release notification requirements of EPCRA Section 304 differ from those of CERCLA Section 103 in some significant respects. For example, reportable releases of CERCLA hazardous substances are also reportable under EPCRA Section 304 (subject to the on-site impact exemption) but reportable releases of EPCRA extremely hazardous substances are not necessarily reportable under CERCLA. Additionally the term "facility" is defined under EPCRA

---

[74] 42 U.S.C. 11001 et seq.

[75] 42 U.S.C. 11004

to include "all" of the equipment and structures at a site thereby requiring an aggregation of releases from different areas of the site in determining whether a release is in a reportable quantity.

EPCRA Section 304 release notifications also must include information regarding the release and its impact that is not required under CERCLA Section 103. Additionally, follow-up reports must be submitted for EPCRA Section 304 releases.

The Clean Water Act includes Section 311[76] which imposes a release notification requirement for releases of oil or hazardous substances in harmful quantities to waters of the United States. Under the statute the person in charge of a vessel or facility from which there is a discharge of oil or hazardous substances to the waters of the United States in a harmful quantity must immediately notify the National Response Center.

The Clean Water Act Section 311 release notification requirements are applicable to releases in harmful quantities to the "navigable waters of the United States" and adjoining shorelines. The term "navigable waters of the United States" has been interpreted to include all waters of the United States over which Congress has the power to regulate interstate commerce. The geographical scope of Section 311 is not limited by the traditional concept of navigability-in-fact but has been construed to extend to virtually all flowing waters including tributaries.

Regulations have been promulgated at 40 CFR Part110 identifying harmful quantities of oil which trigger release notification obligations. Under the regulation an oil spill must be reported if it violates applicable water quality standards or causes a film or sheen on the surface

[76] 33 U.S.C. 1321

of the water or adjoining shoreline or causes a sludge to form. Discharges of oil from properly functioning vessel engines are not considered to be in a harmful quantity.

Pursuant to Section 311 of the Clean Water Act, administrative regulations have been promulgated at 40 CFR Part 112 imposing oil pollution prevention requirements. These regulations require facilities that store certain quantities of oil to develop and implement spill prevention control and countermeasure plans. The regulations also establish implementation procedures for the facility response plans required by larger oil storage facilities under the Oil Pollution Act of 1990.[77]

The hazardous substance release notification requirements of Clean Water Act Section 311 are carried out under administrative regulations codified at 40 CFR Part 116 (identification of hazardous substances) and 40 CFR Part 117 (determination of harmful quantities). The Clean Water Act Section 311 release notification requirements for hazardous substances are similar to the release notification requirements applicable to hazardous substances under CERCLA Section 103; however 40 CFR 117.12 exempts from the notification requirement discharges that are in compliance with NPDES permits.

A number of other federal environmental regulatory programs impose release reporting obligations. Those programs include the hazardous waste management regulations under the Resource Conservation and Recovery Act, the underground storage tank program (UST) under 40 CFR Part 280, regulations promulgated under the Hazardous Materials Transportation Act,[78] and the polychlorinated biphenyl (PCB) and substantial risk provisions of the Toxic Substances

---

[77] Pub. L. 101-380

[78] 49 U.S.C. 5101 et seq.

Control Act[79]. Remediation requirements of those programs are addressed more extensively in the chapters regarding those programs.

Kentucky's release notification requirements are generally consistent with the requirements applicable under federal law but expand upon them in certain respects. KRS 224.01-400, Kentucky's counterpart to CERCLA, establishes the basic release notification requirements in Kentucky. The statute incorporates by reference the release notification requirements for hazardous substances under 40 CFR Part 302 (CERCLA Section 103) and for extremely hazardous substances under 40 CFR Part 355 (EPCRA Section 304) and requires notification of such releases to be provided to NREPC's emergency response center.

The state statute also requires notification of the release to the environment of pollutants or contaminants (other than hazardous substances and extremely hazardous substances) in quantities which may present an imminent or substantial danger to the environment. The term "pollutant or contaminant" is defined very broadly to include virtually any substance that has the potential to adversely affect the environment.

Under the statute NREPC has the authority, by regulation, to identify pollutants or contaminants, to change the lists of hazardous substances and extremely hazardous substances, and to change the reportable quantities. NREPC has not exercised this authority.

KRS 224.01-400 also establishes release reporting requirements for releases of petroleum and petroleum products. The statute requires notification of NREPC's emergency response center whenever an oil spill triggers the oil spill notification requirement of Section 311 of the Clean Water Act. Additionally, it requires notification of the release to the environment of

---

79 15 U.S.C. 2601 et seq.

twenty-five gallons or more of non-diesel petroleum within a twenty-four hour period or the release of seventy-five gallons or more of diesel fuel within such timeframe.

In addition to the other differences noted above, the state notification requirements differ from the federal requirements in other limited respects. For example, the federal law imposes the reporting requirement on the "person in charge" of the vessel or facility from which the release occurred whereas the state law imposes the reporting requirement (except for oil spills reportable under Section 311 of the Clean Water Act) on the "person possessing or controlling" the hazardous substance, extremely hazardous substance, pollutant or contaminant or petroleum. Additionally, the state law requires the reporting of a "threatened release" in a reportable quantity. The state statute's definition does not clarify the meaning of the term "threatened release".

Although KRS 224.01-400 establishes the principal release reporting requirements under Kentucky law, there are reporting requirements under other regulatory authorities. Administrative regulation 401 KAR 5:015 provides that, whenever by emergency or accident a spill or discharge occurs from a sewage system or from a pipeline or container used to transport or store material that would result in or contribute to water pollution, the person in charge of the activity must immediately notify the NREPC Division of Water. The regulation is not limited by reference to a list of specific substances or to specific quantities released. Since the regulation was in effect long before the enactment of KRS 224.01-400 specifying substances and quantities for which releases must be reported, it is possible that the regulation may have been impliedly repealed or modified by the enactment of the statute.

Administrative regulation 401 KAR 50:055 requires that, whenever air emissions due to malfunction, startup, or shutdown may exceed applicable standards, the owner or operator of the source must notify the NREPC DAQ as promptly as possible and submit a follow-up report if requested by the director of the Division. Although the primary purpose of 401 KAR 50:055 is to provide a defense against enforcement when a release results from an excusable malfunction, the regulation has been construed by the agency to impose an affirmative obligation to notify the Division of releases within the scope of the regulation.

B. Release Remediation

Releases to the environment in Kentucky are subject to remediation under both federal and state programs. At the federal level, CERCLA is the general legal authority addressing remediation of such releases. CERCLA is frequently referred to as Superfund, because of the fund created under the law to finance the cleanup program. At the state level, KRS 224.01-400 is the primary remediation statute. Under both federal and state law, other remediation authorities are applicable to specific activities.

CERCLA was enacted in 1980 and amended in 1986 by the Superfund Amendments and Reauthorization Act (SARA)[80] which included the EPCRA provisions that were previously discussed. Under CERCLA, USEPA is authorized to remove or undertake remedial action whenever the release or a substantial threat of a release of hazardous substances, pollutants or contaminants into the environment may present an imminent and substantial endangerment to the public health or welfare. USEPA may conduct the removal or remedial action itself and seek recovery of its costs from persons liable under the statute or USEPA may require such persons to conduct the removal or remediation.

---

80 42 U.S.C. 11001 et seq.

Hazardous substances, the releases of which are subject to removal or remediation under CERCLA, are identified in 40 CFR Part 302, discussed above regarding release notification. It should be noted that removal or remedial action under CERCLA is not limited to releases that are in a reportable quantity. The term "hazardous substance" as used in CERCLA does not include petroleum or hazardous substances that are natural components of petroleum and petroleum products. The term does include, however, hazardous substances that are added to or become mixed with petroleum as a result of its use.

Under CERCLA, liability for removal or remediation costs are imposed on the (1) present owner of the facility to be remediated and persons who owned the facility at the time of or subsequent to the release; (2) persons who generated the hazardous substance and arranged for the transportation or disposal of the material; and (3) transporters of material who selected the site for disposal of the material. Although CERCLA itself is silent as to its retroactive liability, the courts have uniformly held that it applies to conditions that arose prior to enactment of the statute.

USEPA has promulgated at 40 CFR Part 300 a National Contingency Plan (NCP) establishing procedures for response to releases subject to CERCLA. In order for the costs of removal or remediation to be recoverable in private actions under CERCLA, the response action must not be inconsistent with the NCP.

CERCLA provides for the establishment of a National Priority List (NPL) of sites to be remediated under the statute. Sites listed on the NPL are subject to specific procedural requirements to insure that remediation is completed; however, listing on the NPL is not a precondition to remediation pursuant to CERCLA.

Persons potentially liable under CERCLA for the costs of removal or remediation are commonly referred to as potentially responsible parties (PRP). Such persons may include individuals, corporations, partnerships, and governmental entities. Officers and employees of corporate PRPs may be held liable under CERCLA if their duties included responsibility for the activities that gave rise to CERCLA liability. Similarly individual shareholders may be liable as well as corporations if the facts support the "piercing of the corporate veil" under state common law principles. Additionally, corporate parents may be responsible for the CERCLA liability of their corporate subsidiaries if facts support the piercing of the corporate veil under state common law.

CERCLA liability has been construed by the courts to be joint and several among the liable parties except to the extent that liable parties are able to establish the divisibility of the effect of their individual actions. Under the 1986 SARA Amendments to CERCLA, liable parties who incur joint and several liability are entitled to obtain contribution from other liable parties to be determined through consideration of equitable principles under state law.

The courts have held that CERCLA liability is absolute subject to the defenses identified in the statute. Those defenses include (1) act of God, (2) act of war, (3) act of a third party under certain circumstances and (4) an innocent landowner defense. Since CERCLA liability is absolute, it is not based upon fault of the parties and it is not necessary to establish a causal relationship between the activity giving rise to the liability and the response costs that are asserted against the PRP. USEPA has attempted to mitigate the impact of CERCLA liability on lenders by limiting their liability.[81]

---

[81] EPA, Justice Department Policy on CERCLA Enforcement Against Lenders, October 6, 1995

CERCLA Section 107[82] allows private parties to recover from liable parties costs incurred in response to the release or threatened release of hazardous substances. Private cost recovery actions under CERCLA are similar to governmental cost recovery actions provided that the private party establishes that the response costs incurred were not inconsistent with the NCP. One of the principal requirements for consistency with the NCP is public participation in selection of the appropriate remedy.

KRS 224.01-400, Kentucky's mini-Superfund statute, resembles CERCLA in most respects but differs from it in some significant aspects. The state statute was enacted in 1980 while CERCLA was pending before Congress but before the final provisions of CERCLA had been determined. As a result some concepts of CERCLA such as joint and several liability are not clearly addressed in the state statute. Additionally, the issue of retroactive application of the statue is a matter of legal doubt in view of KRS 446.080 which prohibits retroactive applicability of statutes without express statutory authorization.

KRS 224.01-400 was amended in 1992 to confirm that remediation conducted pursuant to the statute could be risk-based, to incorporate provisions protecting certain lenders and fiduciaries from liability, and to establish release reporting requirements comparable to those under the federal programs. NREPC promulgated administrative regulations in 1995 establishing procedures for the implementation of the statute, however, the regulations were rejected by the legislative review committees and expired when the Kentucky General Assembly adjourned in April, 1996. Although no administrative regulations implementing KRS 224.01-

---

[82] 42 U.S.C. 9607

400 are currently in effect, NREPC continues to apply informally many of the concepts of the expired 1995 regulations.

One of the principal differences between CERCLA and KRS 224.01-400 involves identification of PRPs. Under the state statute, liability is imposed on persons "possessing or controlling a hazardous substance, pollutant, or contaminant which is released to the environment, or any person who caused a release to the environment of a hazardous substance, pollutant, or contaminant". Unlike CERCLA, KRS 224.01-400 does not specifically identify off-site generators as PRPs.

KRS 224.01-400 requires that all PRPs characterize releases as necessary to determine the effect on the environment and remediate the release as necessary to correct the effect of the release on the environment. If the release is not in a reportable quantity, the PRP can characterize and remediate the release without NREPC supervision unless otherwise required by the agency. Any person who is required to conduct remediation subject to the supervision of NREPC and who does not remove the released material in its entirety must demonstrate to NREPC that the remediation is protective of human health, safety, and the environment considering a variety of factors including an assessment of exposure and risk.

KRS 224.01-400 has no explicit counterpart to the provisions of CERCLA Section 107 that create a private cause of action for recovery of response costs. KRS 224.01-400(25) does provide, however, for defenses to liability, limitations to liability, and rights to contribution to be determined in accordance with CERCLA Sections 107(a) to (d)[83] and 113(f)[84] and with the Clean Water Act as amended.[85]

In addition to its hazardous substance remediation provisions, KRS 224.01-400 also provides for response to environmental emergencies which include discharges of oil and hazardous substances in violation of Section 311 of the Clean Water Act. NREPC is authorized to recover from PRPs its actual and necessary costs of response incurred under the statue including the costs of responding to environmental emergencies.

In 1994 the Kentucky General Assembly enacted KRS 224.01-405 addressing remedial action for releases of petroleum or petroleum products from sources other than underground storage tanks. The statute is generally patterned after KRS 224.01-400 the hazardous substance remediation statute. KRS 224.01-405 directs NREPC to promulgate administrative regulations establishing standards and procedures for the remediation of petroleum releases. The statute authorizes the use of the risk-based remediation options and requirements of KRS 224.01-400(18) to (21) pending the promulgation of regulations applicable to petroleum remediation. NREPC has not yet promulgated regulations under KRS 224.01-405.

---

83 42 U.S.C. 9607(a) to (d)

84 42 U.S.C. 9613

85 33 U.S.C. 1251 et seq.

CHAPTER 10

Enforcement and Administrative Adjudication

Today's businesses are subject to a host of environmental laws, regulations and permits. A violation of just one of the multitude of mandates can result in administrative, civil, criminal penalties and/or imprisonment. This chapter outlines the process and procedures relating to the administrative, civil and criminal enforcement of environmental laws, regulations and permits as well as administrative adjudication of environmental matters in Kentucky.

A. Enforcement Actions

Several levels of government are vested with authority to enforce environmental laws and regulations in Kentucky. The NREPC, specifically the Division for Air Quality, Division of Waste Management, and Division of Water, take the lead role in the enforcement arena, bringing the majority of enforcement actions. USEPA also has authority to enforce federal laws and regulations in Kentucky and most often exercises this authority when violations are serious.

An enforcement action is an action brought by the USEPA or NREPC to punish a person or entity for violations of permit requirements or environmental laws or regulations. The discretion to bring an enforcement action rests primarily at the state level with NREPC, although enforcement actions may also be brought at the federal level by USEPA through a practice termed "overfiling" when the state fails to act. NREPC and USEPA have a myriad of environmental statutes and regulations to enforce. Indeed, a multitude of environmental statutes and regulations have been enacted at all levels of government - federal, state, and local.

Enforcement actions take three forms - civil administrative actions, civil court actions, and criminal actions. Most federal environmental statutes allow USEPA to bring both a civil and a criminal action for a single violation and allow both the NREPC and USEPA to bring actions for that violation. State law violations may also be enforced both civilly and criminally.

Civil liability for most environmental violations is strict, meaning that almost every violation could result, at a minimum, in civil fines. Criminal liability, in contrast, is usually reserved for more serious violations and usually requires a finding that the defendant acted with knowledge. The NREPC and USEPA consider a host of factors in deciding whether to pursue the enforcement action as a civil or criminal action, or both. However, because civil penalties have a lower threshold of proof and also because civil enforcement can be sought in an administrative action instead of the courts, the bulk of enforcement actions are pursued in the civil administrative arena.

NREPC and USEPA have the benefit of several tools which help to ensure effective and efficient enforcement of environmental laws and regulations.

- Inspections: NREPC, typically through a field inspector, is permitted to periodically visit any property to investigate an entity's compliance with Kentucky's environmental laws and regulations or to investigate actual or suspected instances of environmental violations.

- Power of Abatement: NREPC is granted a power of abatement, allowing it to order, after an investigation, a party to cease, abate, or alleviate a condition or activity found to present a danger to the public's health or welfare or likely to result in damage to natural resources.[86] The NREPC may exercise its power of abatement without affording the party a prior hearing. The law requires only that the party be granted a hearing within 10 days after the issuance of the order.

- Blacklisting: USEPA, through some federal environmental laws, is granted the authority to publish a list of repeat offenders of that law. Listed entities are

[86] See KRS 224.10-410.

prohibited from entering into contractual relationships with government entities. Indirect punitive impacts result also, as unlisted companies doing business with government entities are required to show that listed companies do not supply the component parts for their products.

- "Whistle-blower" Protection Provisions: The majority of federal environmental laws contain provisions that impose sanctions on businesses that punish employees who report environmental violations or initiate citizens suits against their employer.

- Citizen suits: Many environmental laws allow private citizens to bring civil suits for violations of that law. As a jurisdictional prerequisite, notice of intent to initiate a citizen suit must be provided to USEPA, the state where the violation occurred and the violator prior to the suit's commencement. Furthermore, citizen suits are typically barred where a federal or state enforcement proceeding is already underway. While such suits do not allow for the recovery of private damages, they do allow the recovery of civil penalties for the benefit of government and litigation costs.

- Bounties: Some federal environmental statutes provide for awards of up to $1000 to any person (other than government employees on official business) who provides information leading to a civil penalty or criminal conviction for the violation of that law.

(1) Civil Enforcement

(a) Civil Administrative Enforcement Actions

Absent a jurisdictional bar[87], less severe violations are most often pursued administratively. A decision by USEPA or NREPC to pursue an enforcement action administratively usually begins with a notice letter. The notice letter may come under many different names, such as demand letter, field citation or notice of violation, depending on the violation and the enforcing agency. This letter provides the recipient with the grounds and details of the alleged violation. Following the notice letter, one of two paths is followed. In most

---

[87] For example, under the Clean Air Act, penalties exceeding $200,000 may not be sought in an administrative action.

circumstances, the parties will enter settlement negotiations. The goal of such negotiations is to arrive at an Agreed Order or, in a federal action, a Consent Agreement and Final Order (CAFO) or Consent Agreement and Consent Order (CACO). The Agreed Order is an agreed upon pact, outlining the actions to be undertaken or stopped to rectify the violation and typically imposes a penalty. A signed Agreed Order has the force of law and cannot be appealed by the parties to it, although it may be appealed by third parties. In the alternative, as in the case of some severe violations, the USEPA or NREPC may forego settlement negotiations and issue a unilateral order mandating that certain conduct be immediately ceased or undertaken.

If the settlement negotiations do not result in a resolution or if the settlement negotiations have been bypassed, the enforcing agency may file an administrative complaint. State administrative actions are held before and filed with Kentucky's Office of Administrative Hearings in Frankfort. Federal administrative actions are held before an Administrative Law Judge in the county where the defendant conducts business, in Atlanta at EPA's regional headquarters, or in Washington, D.C.

Federal administrative procedures are found at 40 CFR Section 22 and Kentucky's administrative procedures can be found at 400 KAR Chapter 1 and 401 KAR 100:010. In a state action, the parties are afforded discovery after which a formal hearing is held before one of four hearing officers from the NREPC Office of Administrative Hearings. At this hearing, the parties may be represented by counsel, take testimony, cross-examine witnesses and make oral or written arguments. At the conclusion of the hearing, the hearing officer prepares a Report and Recommendation for submission to the secretary of the NREPC. A Report and Recommendation is a report explaining the hearing officer's findings of fact and conclusions of law as well as the hearing officer's recommended final order. The secretary, reviews the Report and Recommendation along with any exceptions filed by interested persons within 14 days of the hearing and issues a decision on the matter.

A decision by the administrative law judge or Secretary of the NREPC in Kentucky, may be further appealed to the proper court. State actions can be appealed to the Franklin Circuit Court within 30 days of the entry of the Secretary's final order.[88] Federal appeals can be filed with the hearing clerk at the EPA headquarters in Washington D.C. within 20 days of the judge's decision.

(b) Civil Judicial Enforcement Litigation

If the enforcing agency chooses not to pursue an enforcement action via the administrative process or if negotiations during the administrative process break down, the agency may choose to bring a civil action in court. An example of a statute most commonly enforced through civil litigation is CERCLA. When the choice is made to enforce a matter through litigation, USEPA typically turns matters over to the Department of Justice, while NREPC hands matters over to the Office of Legal Services. Most state actions initiated by the NREPC are filed in Franklin Circuit Court, while federal actions are heard in U.S. District Court.

Civil lawsuits typically seek two forms of relief; injunctive relief and civil penalties. Civil penalties may recover the economic benefit the violator has enjoyed as a result of noncompliance, may punish the violator for its actions, and may recover for damage to the environment. Injunctive relief may direct the violator to cease the unlawful conduct and prohibit future violations.

(2) Criminal Enforcement

---

[88] See KRS 224.10-470.

Historically, environmental laws were enforced virtually exclusively through civil or administrative actions. However, beginning around 1990, a trend developed for the use of criminal procedures to enforce environmental laws. If the alleged violation is substantial, the enforcing agency may refer the matter to the Department of Justice or the Attorney General for criminal enforcement. A criminal proceeding is particularly serious, for it places not only the violating entity at serious financial risk, but also places corporate officers and senior management personnel who control the decisions that cause the violations at personal risk for penalties and/or imprisonment.

In order to be held criminally liable for the violation of an environmental statute or regulation, the violation ordinarily must have been committed with the requisite level of intent. All Kentucky and a majority of federal environmental crime statutes require that a defendant have knowingly violated the law to be held criminally liable for a violation. Knowledge, however, does not require that there have been an intent to violate the law, only that the defendant knew of the actions constituting the violation. Moreover, a willful blindness to the relevant facts is generally considered to meet the requisite level of intent to support criminal enforcement actions.

Some federal environmental statutes allow criminal penalties to be imposed without a finding that the violator acted with knowledge. Under the Clean Air Act, for example criminal penalties and/or imprisonment for a term of up to one year can be imposed for "negligent endangerment." Negligent endangerment is the negligent release of hazardous air pollutants that places another human being in imminent danger of death or serious bodily harm. Some negligent violations of the Clean Water Act can also result in criminal liability. Negligent violations of permit conditions or pretreatment standards are punishable by moderate criminal fines and/or up to one year of imprisonment.

Because civil penalties are more easily established and because civil actions can be pursued administratively, NREPC and USEPA often opt to bring a civil enforcement action even when a violation is knowing. In deciding whether to proceed with a criminal or civil enforcement action, two considerations are paramount, the amount of environmental harm and the culpability of the violator. Factors indicating culpability are; whether the company has past violations, whether the violation was intentional, whether monitoring equipment has been tampered with by employees, whether reports were falsified, whether unpermitted business operations were engaged in and whether the violation was corrected. Criminal enforcement may also be less likely if the violation was discovered during a voluntary environmental audit, because, as explained in the next section, criminal penalties would be lowered or unrecoverable.

(3) Penalty Calculation

If an enforcement action is concluded adversely to the alleged violator, it will generally result in imposition of a civil penalty. The amount of civil penalty sought and imposed is determined by a host of factors. USEPA has developed a series of "civil penalty policies" under the federal statutes it administers to guide the calculation of a civil penalty amount in federal enforcement actions. Although these policy documents do not have the force of law in Kentucky, NREPC's calculations of penalties have, for the most part, considered federal penalty policies.

The starting point from which EPA begins when assessing a penalty is the amount of economic benefit the violator has derived from the violation. Economic benefit includes the amount of money realized by having avoided or deferred expenditures as a result of the violation.

This is often referred to as "removing the fruits of the violation." The penalty is then increased according to the gravity of the case, or the severity of the violation. Penalties may also be decreased based on certain conduct and/or conditions such as the violator's ability to pay, as well as the violator's good faith efforts.

Penalties may also be reduced if the violator agrees to settle the allegations against it and undertake a "supplemental environmental project" (SEP). A SEP is an environmentally beneficial project that the company is not otherwise legally required to carry out. USEPA policy detailing the ability of an alleged violator to reduce penalties through a SEP, describes the types of projects that are eligible, the penalty mitigation appropriate for a particular project, and the terms and conditions for settlements that include SEPs.[89]

In addition to the factors outlined above, environmental penalties are capped pursuant to statute. KRS 224.99-010 provides enforcement authority for violation of Kentucky's environmental statutes and regulations as well as for violations of NREPC permits and orders. This statute sets forth the maximum civil and criminal penalties for state environmental violations. Maximum sanctions range from a low of $50 per day of violation for certain offenses up to $25,000 per day of violation and one to five years of imprisonment for other offenses. Penalties for violations of state regulations adopted by the State Emergency Response Commission pursuant to EPCRA are found at KRS 39E.990.

Maximum penalties for violations of federal laws vary with the statute. First time violations of federal laws can result in penalties of up to $1,000,000 per day of violation (for

---

[89] See EPA Supplemental Environmental Projects Policy, 60 FR 24856, May 10, 1995; revised at 63 FR 24796, May 5, 1998.

corporations) and/or substantial prison time. Following is a list of the relevant penalty provisions for the major federal environmental laws:

- Clean Air Act (CAA) § 113
- Clean Water Act (CWA) § 309
- Resource Conservation of Recovery Act (RCRA) § 3008
- Comprehensive Response Compensation and Liability Act (CERCLA) § 109
- Emergency Planning and Community Right-to-Know Act (EPCRA) § 325

Some relief from exposure to enforcement actions is available through federal audit policies and Kentucky's environmental audit privilege and immunity law. These policies allow for favorable treatment in enforcement actions for violations discovered during a voluntary environmental audit.

A qualifying environmental audit is defined at KRS 224.01-040 as "a voluntary, internal, and comprehensive evaluation of one or more facilities or an activity at one or more facilities regulated under KRS Chapter 224 or federal, regional, or local counterparts, or of management systems related to that facility or activity where the evaluation is designed to identify and prevent non-compliance and to improve compliance with statutory and regulatory requirements."

USEPA's audit policy, effective in 1996, allows civil penalties to be reduced for violations discovered during a voluntary environmental audit and allows for leniency in a corresponding criminal action. Kentucky's law, by contrast, allows, in certain circumstances, complete immunity from civil penalties for violations discovered during such an audit if the violations are voluntarily disclosed to the Cabinet and promptly corrected. Kentucky's law also extends an evidentiary privilege to all evidence of environmental violations discovered during the audit from use in legal proceedings. Kentucky's law, however, has come under much criticism from USEPA and is likely to be amended in the near future to more closely correspond to the comparable federal law.

B. Administrative Adjudication

Regulated entities are not at the complete mercy of those enforcing environmental laws and regulations. Under most circumstances, a regulated entity may appeal an NREPC decision to the NREPC Secretary through the Office of Administrative Hearings or may seek declaratory or injunctive relief from burdensome laws and regulations in court.

Pursuant to Kentucky law, a person who has not been previously heard regarding the issuance of any order or the making of any final determination, may file a petition for an administrative hearing with the NREPC alleging that the determination or order is contrary to law or fact and has caused him injury as a result.[90] A petition may follow the denial, issuance, revocation or modification of an environmental permit or any other action by NREPC or its officials and may be initiated by the permit applicant or by a person or group impacted by the administrative decision. The right to petition for a hearing is available for only thirty days after the petitioner had notice, or could reasonably have had such notice, of the order or final determination complained of.

NREPC's administrative rules of procedure are found at 400 KAR Chapter 1 and 401 KAR 100.010. The process is similar to a typical court proceeding. Following discovery, a formal hearing is held before one of four hearing officers from the NREPC Office of Administrative Hearings. At this hearing, the parties may be represented by counsel, take

---

[90] See KRS 224.10-420(2).

testimony, cross-examine witnesses and make oral or written arguments. At the conclusion of the hearing, the hearing officer prepares a Report and Recommendation for submission to the Secretary of the NREPC. Like administrative enforcement actions, the Secretary then reviews the Report and Recommendation along with any exceptions filed by interested persons within 14 days of the Report and Recommendation and issues an order on the matter.

The order of the Secretary may be further appealed to the Franklin Circuit Court. Such an appeal must be filed within 30 days of the Secretary's order.

If the appeal concerns the issuance of a permit, a motion to stay the permit conditions may be sought. A stay of permit conditions postpones the imposition of the permit requirements until the resolution of the administrative action. Stays are expressly provided for in the case of KPDES permits,[91] and may be implicitly authorized in the case of other permits.

Generally speaking, litigation involving environmental matters is initially filed as an administrative action. However, in certain exceptional circumstances a claimant may turn immediately to the courts for relief from an enforcement action or upon suffering adversely from the imposition of a statute, ordinance, or other governmental regulation.

A general limitation on parties seeking judicial relief from environmental regulations or agency action is the doctrine of exhaustion of administrative remedies which provides that a party may only seek judicial relief after he has sought relief in an administrative action. However, a party may seek judicial relief before administrative proceedings are complete or even initiated at all when the challenge concerns the constitutionality of an agency's actions or a claim that the agency has acted beyond its authority. Furthermore, a party is not required to exhaust its

[91] See 401 KAR 5:075 (11).

administrative remedies where resort to the administrative process would be futile and a viable remedy through the agency no longer exists. Courts have also recognized a right to direct judicial relief where the question at issue is purely legal instead of factual.

If a party has exhausted its administrative remedies or meets one of the exceptions outlined above, an action challenging an enforcement action, environmental law or regulation may be brought in state court. These actions encompass more than just actions challenging the constitutionality of a law. For example, a claimant may request a Declaration of Rights, where an actual controversy exists asking the court to explain the relative rights of the parties. In some instances, a party may turn to the court seeking a temporary injunction in order to maintain existing conditions, or the status quo, pending the outcome of a trial on the merits of a corresponding enforcement action.[92] To prevail on a motion for temporary injunction, the claimant must demonstrate that he will suffer irreparable and immediate harm unless the injunction is granted and must show that the harm to the claimant outweighs the potential harm to the public interest.

---

[92] See Declaratory Judgment Act, 28 U.S.C. §2201 *et seq*. SEE ALSO KRS 418.040

CHAPTER 11

Administrative Rule-Making in Kentucky

Since most environmental regulatory requirements in Kentucky are imposed through administrative regulations rather than statutory enactments, the procedures by which administrative regulations are promulgated constitute an important aspect of environmental law in Kentucky. Administrative rule-making by NREPC is conducted under the procedures specified in KRS Chapter 13A. The statute establishes uniform rule-making procedures applicable to all state agencies; however, the agencies must also comply with any additional procedural or substantive requirements imposed by the statute under which the agency functions.

Under KRS Chapter 13A administrative rule-making (other than emergency regulations) commences with the publication by the promulgating agency of a Notice of Intent in the Administrative Register of Kentucky, a monthly publication of the Legislative Research Commission. The Notice of Intent consists of a brief summary of the issue on which the agency intends to conduct rule-making and the time and place at which comments on the issue may be presented to the agency. The agency may have prepared a draft regulation at this point, but usually will not have done so. The Notice of Intent is equivalent to an advance notice of proposed rule-making under federal rule-making procedures in that it is intended to elicit input from interested parties but does not formally initiate the rule-making process. The agency must conduct a non-adversarial public hearing on the Notice of Intent; however the agency may cancel the public hearing if no one indicates a desire to participate in the hearing. Within forty-five days after the public hearing, the agency must issue a Statement of Consideration setting forth the agency's response to comments submitted on the Notice of Intent.

After completion of the Notice of Intent procedure, the administrative agency initiates the formal rule-making process by filing with the Legislative Research Commission a proposed administrative regulation and supporting information. The supporting information must include data regarding the public hearing on the proposed regulation, a regulatory impact analysis, a fiscal note, a tiering statement, and a federal mandate analysis. The supporting information serves the purpose of the preamble to federal rule-making in that it provides information regarding the basis for rule-making, the options considered by the agency and its anticipated effect. The Legislative Research Commission publishes the proposed administrative regulation and the supporting information in the Administrative Register.

The administrative agency will conduct a public hearing on the proposed regulation between twenty and thirty days after publication of the proposal in the Administrative Register. The public hearing is non-adversarial in that testimony is not submitted under oath and cross-examination of witnesses is not permitted. Testimony may take the form of an oral presentation or it may be submitted in written form.

In addition to the administrative rule-making procedures applicable to all other administrative agencies in Kentucky, NREPC must receive and consider the recommendations of its advisory body, the Kentucky Environmental Quality Commission, after public hearing and before promulgation of the regulation. KRS 224.01-115 provides that the Cabinet must provide the Environmental Quality Commission with a written explanation of its action if it proceeds with a regulatory promulgation contrary to the recommendation of the Commission.

Administrative agencies must file with the Legislative Research Commission a Statement of Consideration in response to comments submitted on the proposed administrative regulation along with the administrative regulation as revised to reflect any changes arising from the public hearing process. The agency must take such action within fifteen days following the public hearing but may extend the deadline for an additional thirty days. If the regulation has been revised after the public hearing, the revised regulation must again be published in the Administrative Register.

After the administrative agency has completed its action on the proposed administrative regulation, the focus of the administrative rule-making process shifts to the Kentucky General Assembly. The proposed regulation is first reviewed by the Administrative Regulation Review Subcommittee (ARRS) of the Legislative Research Commission. ARRS is composed of both senators and representatives and it reviews the proposed administrative regulation as to its consistency with statutory authority and legislative intent. Additionally ARRS reviews the procedures utilized by the administrative agency in the rule-making process as to their compliance with KRS Chapter 13A. ARRS conducts its review in meetings open to the public and with the opportunity for the public to present views on the issue.

If ARRS approves the proposed regulation, the regulation is referred by the Legislative Research Commission to the joint House-Senate committee having jurisdiction over the subject matter. Environmental regulations are referred to the Interim Joint Committee on Agriculture and Natural Resources. The jurisdictional committee conducts the same type of review that was conducted by the ARRS. If the proposed regulation is approved by the ARRS and the jurisdictional committee, the administrative regulation becomes effective upon the adjournment of the meeting of the jurisdictional committee.

Neither ARRS nor the jurisdictional committee has the authority to prevent or delay the administrative regulation from taking effect; however, the proposed regulation may be amended before ARRS or the jurisdictional committee with the approval of the promulgating agency either upon the request of the legislative committee or of the promulgating agency itself.

If ARRS or the jurisdictional committee finds the proposed administrative regulation to be deficient, the governor may determine that the regulation shall take effect notwithstanding the finding of deficiency. If a regulation that has been found deficient by a legislative committee is put into effect by the governor, the regulation will "sunset" and expire at the adjournment of the next regular session of the Kentucky General Assembly unless the regulation has been enacted as a statute by the Kentucky General Assembly or unless the objecting legislative committee has withdrawn its deficiency determination.

Emergency administrative regulations may be put into effect without compliance with the administrative rule-making procedures of KRS Chapter 13A. Emergency administrative regulations take effect upon filing and can remain in effect for one hundred seventy days except under certain limited circumstances. Emergency administrative regulations are published in the Administrative Register and can not be renewed for a period of time after its filing.

APPENDIX A

This appendix consists of a description by the NREPC Department for Environmental Protection of the permit programs administered by agencies within the department.

INTRODUCTION

The Natural Resources and Environmental Protection Cabinet is responsible for the protection and preservation of Kentucky's land, air, and water resources. Created originally to conserve, maintain, and preserve our land and water resources, the Cabinet is the chief agency also responsible for the prevention, abatement, and control of all water, land, and air pollution and the reclamation of lands adversely affected by surface and underground mining.

The Cabinet is divided into three departments - Environmental Protection, Natural Resources, and Surface Mining Reclamation and Enforcement. Each department is charged with specific responsibilities to carry out the Cabinet's various programs.

This document focuses on the permitting programs administered by the Department for Environmental Protection. The Department's permitting system allows for the control of air emissions, water withdrawals and discharges, and management of wastes in such a way as to protect the public and our environment. Information on the Department's permit requirements and application procedures are contained in this document and are updated yearly. Additional information or detailed instructions on applying for the environmental permits issued by this agency may be obtained from:

Department for Environmental Protection
Commissioner's Office
% Margaret Shanks
14 Reilly Road
Frankfort, Kentucky 40601
Telephone: (502) 564-2150
Fax: (502) 564-4245

This document can also be viewed through the Internet: The address is:

http://www.state.ky.us/agencies/nrepc/nrepc/epa/prtocl.htm

In addition, information concerning specific permit applications can be viewed through the Public Index System at:

http://www.state.ky.us/agencies/nrepc/public/pix_main.htm

DEPARTMENT FOR ENVIRONMENTAL PROTECTION S PERMIT COORDINATION PROCESS

For assistance in obtaining necessary state-level environmental permits and to improve coordination of the Department for Environmental Protection's permitting processes for projects requiring multiple permits, contact Margaret Shanks at (502) 564-2150.

The permits coordinator can provide the following:

1. Serve as a central contact for applicants to obtain permit application information including permit application forms and how to obtain copies of current regulations;
2. Assist in identifying, based on information supplied by the applicant, all Department permit and registration requirements and outlines the probable steps and times involved to secure the permits;
3. Coordinate pre-application conferences between the applicant and the Department; and,
4. Provide for Department coordination during the permit application review process and can respond to applicant inquiries concerning the Department review process.

These services will not eliminate or modify any requirement set out by Kentucky statutes or regulations but will aid the applicant at the initial stages of project planning by identifying all Department permits, registrations, or approvals that could be required for a project. This process provides the applicant and other individuals a central contact point for Department information and thus a better understanding of the state's environmental permitting processes. A considerable amount of time and correspondence formerly needed between the applicant and the Department has now been eliminated by this coordination process.

DOCUMENT OVERVIEW AND PERMIT CHECKLIST

The Department for Environmental Protection is responsible for maintaining the quality of Kentucky's land, air, and water resources and public and semi-public drinking water supplies. To accomplish this task, the Department regulates sources of air and water pollution, public and semi-public water treatment facilities, sewage treatment plants, and the management of hazardous and non-hazardous waste. These responsibilities are carried out by three divisions of the Department - Division for Air Quality, Division of Waste Management, and Division of Water.

This document contains detailed information concerning all Department permits, registrations, and approvals. Information on programs that do not involve permitting can be obtained by contacting the Department.

Each permit (registration or approval) is discussed in the following standard format:

A. **Legal Authority:** The statute or regulation authorizing the issuance of the permit is identified. Included are the appropriate sections of Kentucky law from *Kentucky Revised Statutes (KRS)* and the appropriate citations from the *Kentucky Administrative Regulations (KAR)*.
B. **Permit, Registration, Approval, or Certification Requirements:** Under what conditions the permit is required.
C. **Time Limits:** For a majority of the permits, time limits for permit application processing are set by regulation or statute. If there is no time limit set, applications will be processed within various time frames depending on each division's workload.
D. **Fees:** The fee charged for the permit.
E. **Forms:** The Department form number, when applicable, and application title are provided.
F. **Procedures:** Procedures for applying for the permit are described, including the time interval for public notification if required.
G. **Permit, Registration, Approval, or Certification Duration:** The effective term of the permit.

A listing of all Department permits (registrations and approvals) described in this document is contained on the following pages. This checklist serves as the first step in identifying the environmental permits that may be required for a proposed facility. Once the permit is identified, the applicant should refer to the appropriate section in this document for detailed information (see Table of Contents for page number).

DEPARTMENT FOR ENVIRONMENTAL PROTECTION CHECKLIST FOR ENVIRONMENTAL PERMITS

DIVISION REQUIRING PERMIT	NAME OF PERMIT (Registration or Approval)	REQUIREMENTS
Division for Air Quality	1. Air Permit	Construction/operation of an air contaminant source and its air pollution control equipment.
	2. Notification to Remove Asbestos	Asbestos removal activities subject to 401 KAR 57:011.
	3. Gasoline Tank Truck Certification	Certification for the control of volatile organic compound emissions from leaks from gasoline tank trucks.
Division of Waste Management	1. Solid Waste Landfill Permit a. Contained Landfill b. Construction/Demolition Debris Landfill c. Residual Landfill	Construction and operation of a solid waste disposal facility for disposal of non-hazardous waste, also household hazardous waste and limited quantity generator hazardous waste for contained landfill.
	2. Landfarming Permit	Operation of a landfarming facility for sludge application to agricultural land.
	3. Registered Permit-By-Rule	Required for a limited number of solid and special waste facilities– See 401 KAR 47:080, Section 2(6).
	4. Solid and Special Waste Emergency Permit	For short-term storage or disposal of a solid or special waste generated from an emergency such as a storm or flood.
	5. Research, Development, and Demonstration Permit	For demonstration projects of new or unproven technology.
	6. Hazardous Waste Generator Registration	Production of more than 100 kilograms of non-acute or 1 kilogram of acutely hazardous waste per month.
	7. Hazardous Waste Transporter Registration	Transportation of hazardous waste within the Commonwealth of Kentucky.
	8. Hazardous Waste Recycler Registration	Recycling hazardous wastes.
	9. Hazardous Waste Facility Permit a. Storage b. Treatment c. Disposal	Construction and operation of a facility for the storage of hazardous waste or storage by a hazardous waste generator for more than 90 days, for the treatment of hazardous waste, or for the disposal of hazardous waste. For post-closure care and monitoring of hazardous waste disposal facilities.
	10. Hazardous Waste Emergency Permit	Temporary treatment, storage, or disposal of hazardous waste in an emergency.
DIVISION REQUIRING PERMIT	**NAME OF PERMIT (Registration or Approval)**	**REQUIREMENTS**
	11. Hazardous Waste Research, Development, and Demonstration Permit	Hazardous waste treatment facility engaged in experimental activities.
	12. Underground Storage Tank Notification and Closure	Installation, closure, or existence of an underground storage tank.

DIVISION REQUIRING PERMIT	NAME OF PERMIT (Registration or Approval)	REQUIREMENTS
	13. Used Oil Registration	Recycling of more than 5,000 gallons, transporting more than 500 gallons, or storing more than 10,000 gallons of used oil annually.
Division of Water	1. Wastewater Facility Construction Permit	Construction or modification of any facility for the treatment of wastewater. (Not required for industrial wastewater treatment plants.)
	2. Kentucky Pollutant Discharge Elimination System (KPDES) Permit	Discharge of pollutants from any point source into waters of the Commonwealth.
	3. KPDES Stormwater Discharge Permit– Construction and Operating Activities	Discharge of stormwater from point sources into waters of the Commonwealth.
	4. No Discharge Operational Permit	Operation of a closed circuit, subsurface injection, or land application wastewater system.
	5. Kentucky Inter-Municipal Operational Permit	Operation of a publicly owned sewer system with 5,000 linear feet or more of sewer line that discharges to a sewer system or wastewater treatment plant owned by another system.
	6. Floodplain Construction Permit	Construction in, along, or across the floodplain of any stream in the Commonwealth except those included in surface mining permits.
	7. Dam Construction Permit	Construction of a dam in excess of 25 feet tall or 50 acre-feet of storage except those included in surface coal mining permits.
	8. Wild Rivers Permit a. Utility Right-of-Way Construction Permit b. Change-of-Use Permit	Construction of a transmission line or pipeline right-of-way within any portion of a wild river corridor.
	9. Water Withdrawal Permit	Withdrawal or diversion of more than 10,000 gallons per day of water from a surface or sub-surface source.
	10. Oil and Gas Facilities a. Oil and Gas Facility Registration b. Holding Pit Construction Permit c. Produced Water Transport Approval	a. Facilities that cause or are capable of causing produced water. b. Construction of a produced water holding pit. c. Transportation of produced water away from a facility where it is produced.
	11. Approval of Municipal Pretreatment Program	Municipalities that have significant industrial users discharging wastewater into the municipal system.

	12. Approvals a. Approval to Construct Public Water Supply Facilities b. Approval to Impound c. Approval to Construct or Modify Sewer Lines, Pump Stations, or Force Mains d. Section 401 Water Quality Certification	a. Construction of public water supply facilities. b. Impounding water behind a dam. c. Sewer line extensions to publicly owned treatment works or private plants, or modification of existing facilities. d. Any discharge into the waters of the Commonwealth associated with any federally licensed or permitted activity.

APPENDIX B

This appendix consists of the organizational charts of the Natural Resources and Environmental Protection Cabinet, the Cabinet's Department for Environmental Protection, the Department's Division of Water and the Department's Division for Air Quality.

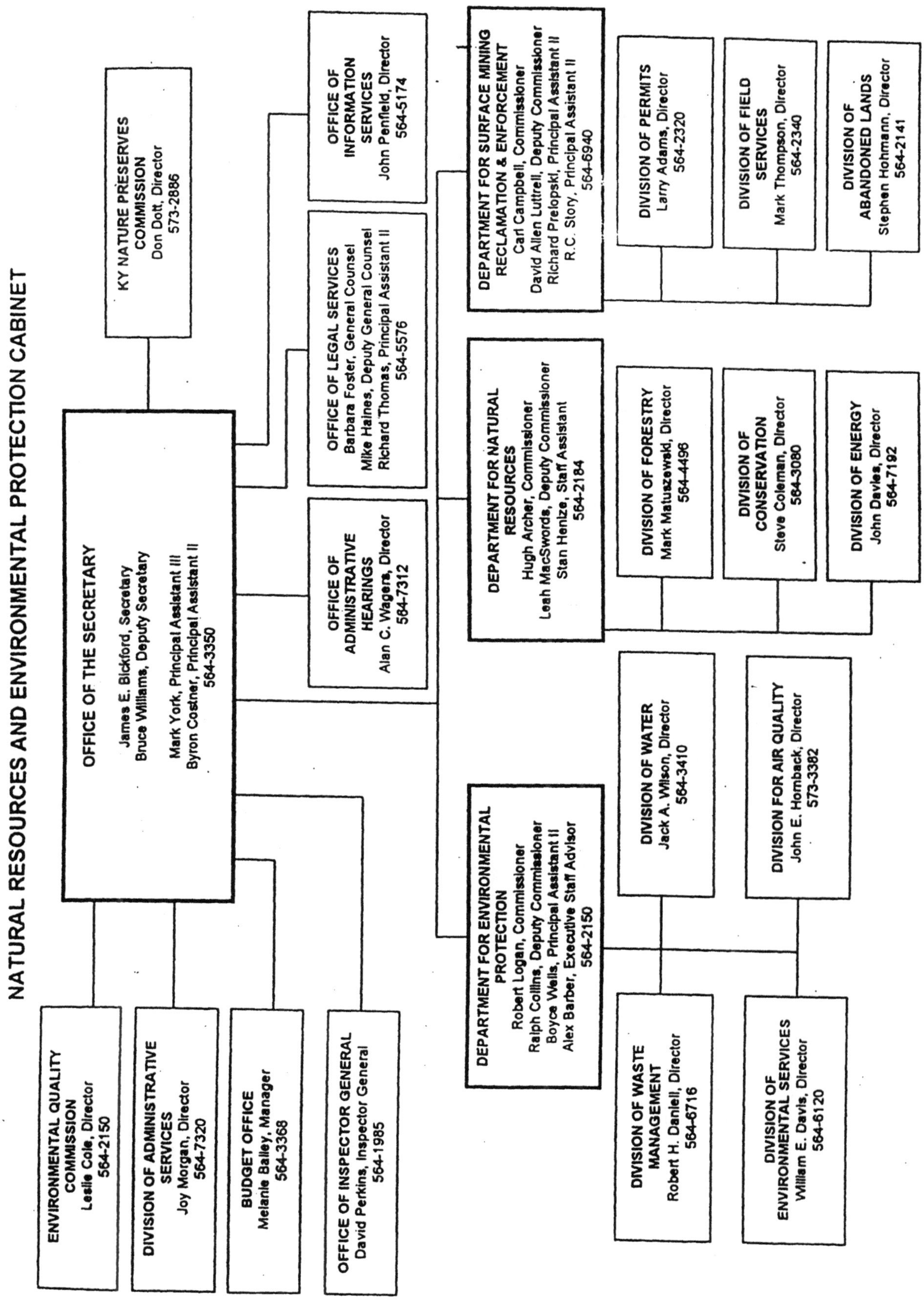
NATURAL RESOURCES AND ENVIRONMENTAL PROTECTION CABINET
KY NATURE PRESERVES COMMISSION
Don Dott, Director
573-2886
OFFICE OF THE SECRETARY
James E. Bickford, Secretary
Bruce Williams, Deputy Secretary
Mark York, Principal Assistant III
Byron Costner, Principal Assistant II
564-3350
ENVIRONMENTAL QUALITY COMMISSION
Leslie Cole, Director
564-2150
DIVISION OF ADMINISTRATIVE SERVICES
Joy Morgan, Director
564-7320
BUDGET OFFICE
Melanie Bailey, Manager
564-3368
OFFICE OF INSPECTOR GENERAL
David Perkins, Inspector General
564-1985
OFFICE OF INFORMATION SERVICES
John Penfield, Director
564-5174
OFFICE OF LEGAL SERVICES
Barbara Foster, General Counsel
Mike Haines, Deputy General Counsel
Richard Thomas, Principal Assistant II
564-5576
OFFICE OF ADMINISTRATIVE HEARINGS
Alan C. Wagers, Director
564-7312
DEPARTMENT FOR SURFACE MINING RECLAMATION & ENFORCEMENT
Carl Campbell, Commissioner
David Allen Luttrell, Deputy Commissioner
Richard Prelopski, Principal Assistant II
R.C. Story, Principal Assistant II
564-6940
DIVISION OF PERMITS
Larry Adams, Director
564-2320
DIVISION OF FIELD SERVICES
Mark Thompson, Director
564-2340
DIVISION OF ABANDONED LANDS
Stephen Hohmann, Director
564-2141
DEPARTMENT FOR NATURAL RESOURCES
Hugh Archer, Commissioner
Leah MacSwords, Deputy Commissioner
Stan Henize, Staff Assistant
564-2184
DIVISION OF FORESTRY
Mark Matuszewski, Director
564-4496
DIVISION OF CONSERVATION
Steve Coleman, Director
564-3080
DIVISION OF ENERGY
John Davies, Director
564-7192
DEPARTMENT FOR ENVIRONMENTAL PROTECTION
Robert Logan, Commissioner
Ralph Collins, Deputy Commissioner
Boyce Wells, Principal Assistant II
Alex Barber, Executive Staff Advisor
564-2150
DIVISION OF WATER
Jack A. Wilson, Director
564-3410
DIVISION FOR AIR QUALITY
John E. Hornback, Director
573-3382
DIVISION OF WASTE MANAGEMENT
Robert H. Daniell, Director
564-6716
DIVISION OF ENVIRONMENTAL SERVICES
William E. Davis, Director
564-6120

NATURAL RESOURCES AND ENVIRONMENTAL PROTECTION CABINET
DEPARTMENT FOR ENVIRONMENTAL PROTECTION

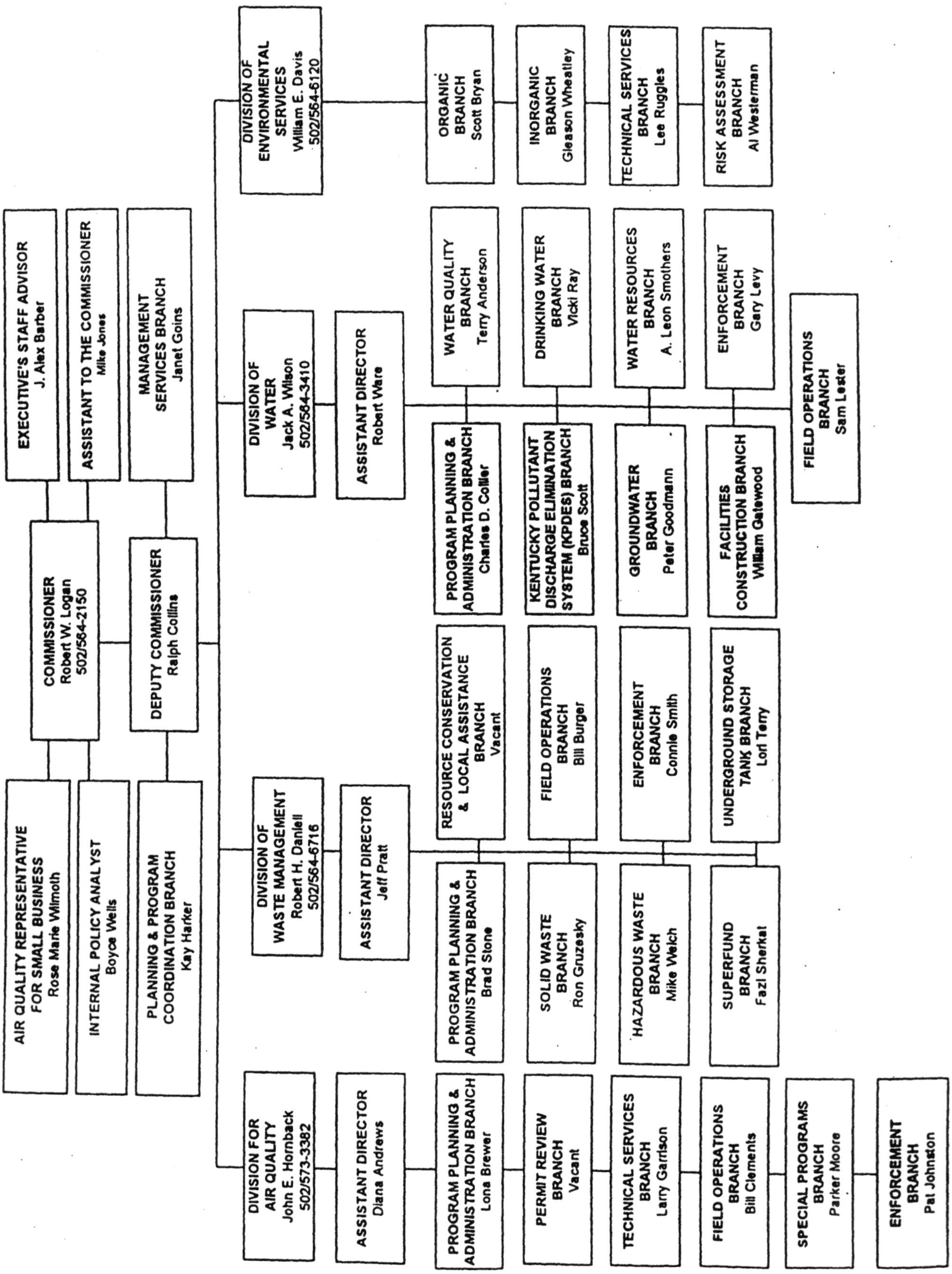

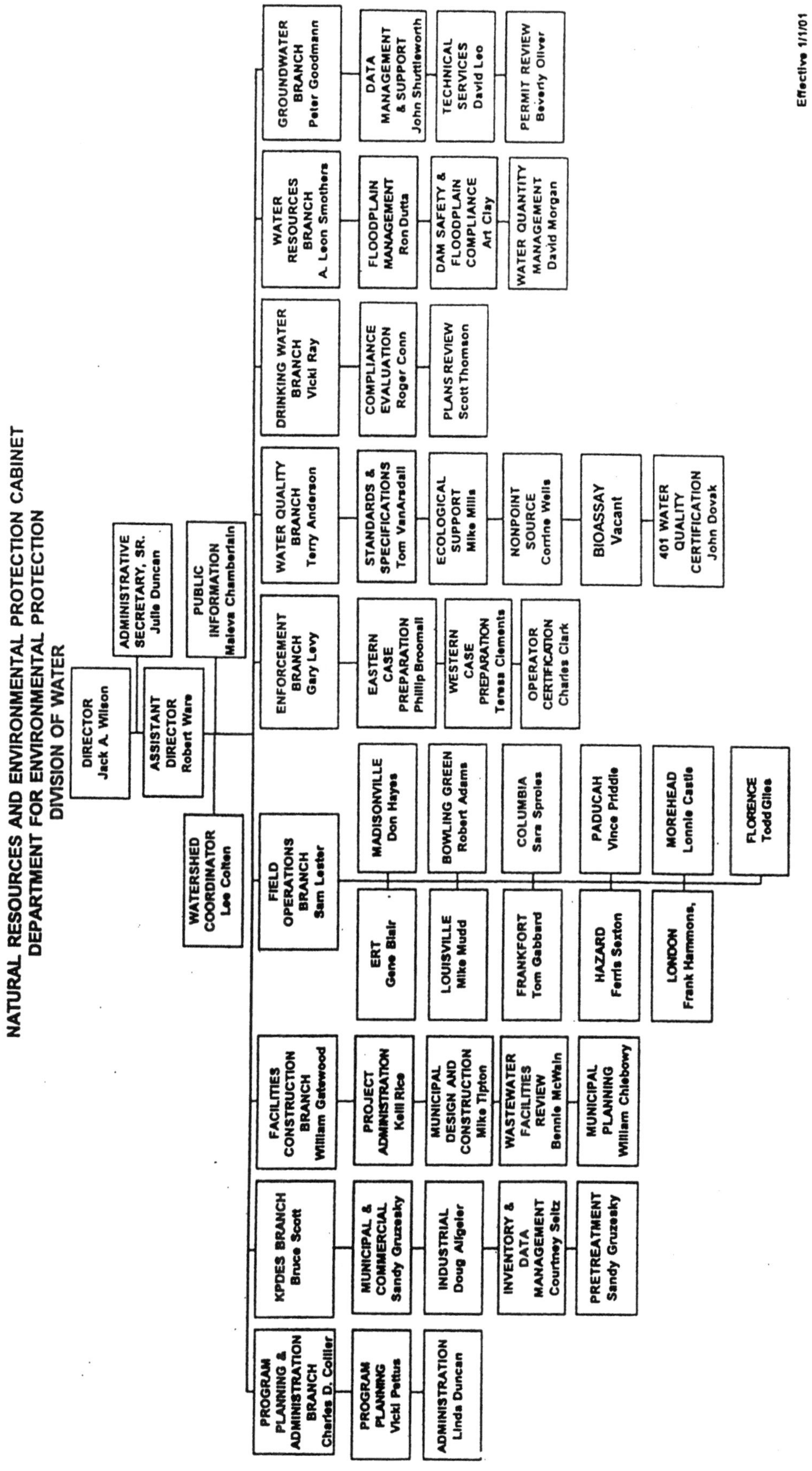
NATURAL RESOURCES AND ENVIRONMENTAL PROTECTION CABINET
DEPARTMENT FOR ENVIRONMENTAL PROTECTION
DIVISION OF WATER
DIRECTOR Jack A. Wilson
ADMINISTRATIVE SECRETARY, SR. Julie Duncan
ASSISTANT DIRECTOR Robert Ware
PUBLIC INFORMATION Maleva Chamberlain
WATERSHED COORDINATOR Lee Colten
PROGRAM PLANNING & ADMINISTRATION BRANCH Charles D. Collier
PROGRAM PLANNING Vicki Pettus
ADMINISTRATION Linda Duncan
KPDES BRANCH Bruce Scott
MUNICIPAL & COMMERCIAL Sandy Gruzesky
INDUSTRIAL Doug Allgeier
INVENTORY & DATA MANAGEMENT Courtney Seitz
PRETREATMENT Sandy Gruzesky
FACILITIES CONSTRUCTION BRANCH William Gatewood
PROJECT ADMINISTRATION Kelli Rice
MUNICIPAL DESIGN AND CONSTRUCTION Mike Tipton
WASTEWATER FACILITIES REVIEW Bennie McWain
MUNICIPAL PLANNING William Chlebowy
FIELD OPERATIONS BRANCH Sam Lester
ERT Gene Blair
LOUISVILLE Mike Mudd
FRANKFORT Tom Gabbard
HAZARD Ferris Sexton
LONDON Frank Hammons,
MADISONVILLE Don Hayes
BOWLING GREEN Robert Adams
COLUMBIA Sara Sproles
PADUCAH Vince Priddle
MOREHEAD Lonnie Castle
FLORENCE Todd Giles
ENFORCEMENT BRANCH Gary Levy
EASTERN CASE PREPARATION Phillip Broomall
WESTERN CASE PREPARATION Teresa Clements
OPERATOR CERTIFICATION Charles Clark
WATER QUALITY BRANCH Terry Anderson
STANDARDS & SPECIFICATIONS Tom VanArsdall
ECOLOGICAL SUPPORT Mike Mills
NONPOINT SOURCE Corrine Wells
BIOASSAY Vacant
401 WATER QUALITY CERTIFICATION John Dovak
DRINKING WATER BRANCH Vicki Ray
COMPLIANCE EVALUATION Roger Conn
PLANS REVIEW Scott Thomson
WATER RESOURCES BRANCH A. Leon Smothers
FLOODPLAIN MANAGEMENT Ron Dutta
DAM SAFETY & FLOODPLAIN COMPLIANCE Art Clay
WATER QUANTITY MANAGEMENT David Morgan
GROUNDWATER BRANCH Peter Goodmann
DATA MANAGEMENT & SUPPORT John Shuttleworth
TECHNICAL SERVICES David Leo
PERMIT REVIEW Beverly Oliver
Effective 1/1/01

Natural Resources and Environmental Protection Cabinet
Department for Environmental Protection
Division for Air Quality
803 Schenkel Lane
Frankfort, KY 40601
Telephone: (502) 573-3382 Fax: (502) 573-3787

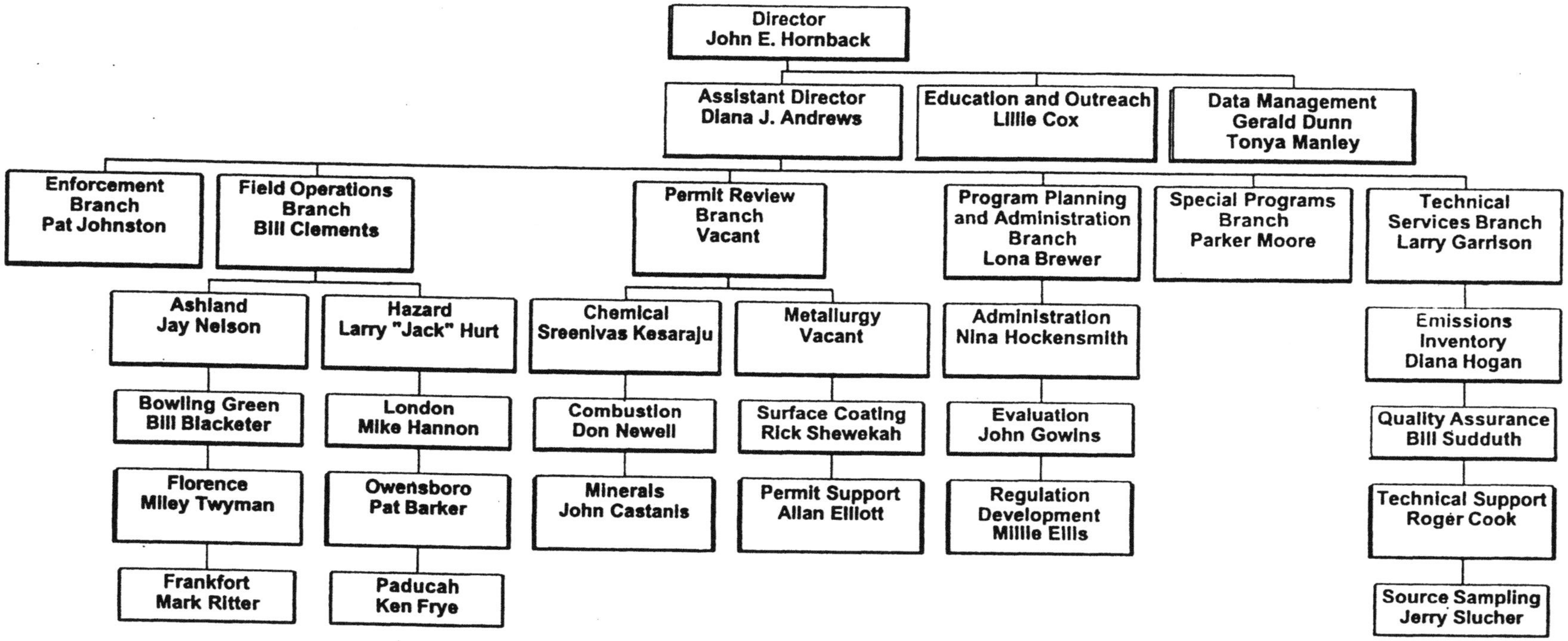

Revised 01/25/01

Government Institutes Mini-Catalog

PC #	ENVIRONMENTAL TITLES	Pub Date	Price*
629	ABCs of Environmental Regulation: Understanding the Fed Regs	1998	$65
672	Book of Lists for Regulated Hazardous Substances, 9th Edition	1999	$95
4100	CFR Chemical Lists on CD ROM, 1999-2000 Edition	1999	$125
512	Clean Water Handbook, 2nd Edition	1996	$115
581	EH&S Auditing Made Easy	1997	$95
673	E H & S CFR Training Requirements, 4th Edition	2000	$99
525	Environmental Audits, 7th Edition	1996	$95
548	Environmental Engineering and Science: An Introduction	1997	$95
643	Environmental Guide to the Internet, 4th Edition	1998	$75
650	Environmental Law Handbook, 15th Edition	1999	$89
688	EH&S Dictionary: Official Regulatory Terms, 7th Edition	2000	$95
676	Environmental Statutes, 2000 Edition	2000	$105
570	ESAs Made Easy	1996	$75
707	Federal Facility Environmental Compliance and Enforcement Guide	2000	$115
708	Federal Facility Environmental Management Systems	2000	$99
689	Fundamentals of Site Remediation	2000	$85
515	Industrial Environmental Management: A Practical Approach	1996	$95
510	ISO 14000: Understanding Environmental Standards	1996	$85
551	ISO 14001: An Executive Report	1996	$75
588	International Environmental Auditing	1998	$179
518	Lead Regulation Handbook	1996	$95
608	NEPA Effectiveness: Mastering the Process	1998	$95
582	Recycling & Waste Mgmt Guide to the Internet	1997	$65
615	Risk Management Planning Handbook	1998	$105
603	Superfund Manual, 6th Edition	1997	$129
685	State Environmental Agencies on the Internet	1999	$75
566	TSCA Handbook, 3rd Edition	1997	$115
534	Wetland Mitigation: Mitigation Banking and Other Strategies	1997	$95

PC #	SAFETY and HEALTH TITLES	Pub Date	Price*
697	Applied Statistics in Occuapational Safety and Health	2000	$105
547	Construction Safety Handbook	1996	$95
553	Cumulative Trauma Disorders	1997	$75
663	Forklift Safety, 2nd Edition	1999	$85
709	Fundamentals of Occupational Safety & Health, 2nd Edition	2001	$69
612	HAZWOPER Incident Command	1998	$75
535	Making Sense of OSHA Compliance	1997	$75
662	Machine Guarding Handbook	1999	$75
718	OSHA's New Ergonomic Standard	2001	$95
558	PPE Made Easy	1998	$95
683	Product Safety Handbook: The Mfgr.'s Guide to Legal Requirements	2001	$95
598	Project Mgmt for E H & S Professionals	1997	$85
658	Root Cause Analysis	1999	$105
552	Safety & Health in Agriculture, Forestry and Fisheries	1997	$155
669	Safety & Health on the Internet, 3rd Edition	1999	$75
668	Safety Made Easy, 2nd	1999	$75
590	Your Company Safety and Health Manual	1997	$95

Government Institutes Order Form

4 Research Place, Suite 200 • Rockville, MD 20850-3226
Tel (301) 921-2323 • Fax (301) 921-0264
Internet: http://www.govinst.com • E-mail: giinfo@govinst.com

4 EASY WAYS TO ORDER

1. Tel: **(301) 921-2323**
Have your credit card ready when you call.

2. Fax: **(301) 921-0264**
Fax this completed order form with your company purchase order or credit card information.

3. Mail: **Government Institutes Division**
ABS Group Inc.
P.O. Box 846304
Dallas, TX 75284-6304 USA
Mail this completed order form with a check, company purchase order, or credit card information.

4. Online: **Visit http://www.govinst.com**

PAYMENT OPTIONS

❑ **Check** *(payable in US dollars to **ABS Group Inc. Government Institutes Division**)*

❑ **Purchase Order** *(This order form must be attached to your company P.O. Note: All International orders must be prepaid.)*

❑ **Credit Card** ❑ VISA ❑ MasterCard ❑ American Express

Exp. ___ /____

Credit Card No. ______________________

Signature ______________________

(Government Institutes' Federal I.D.# is 13-2695912)

CUSTOMER INFORMATION

Ship To: (Please attach your purchase order)

Name ______________________

GI Account # *(7 digits on mailing label)* ______________________

Company/Institution ______________________

Address ______________________
(Please supply street address for UPS shipping)

____

City ____________ State/Province ____________

Zip/Postal Code ____________ Country ____________

Tel ( ) ______________________

Fax ( ) ______________________

Email Address ______________________

Bill To: (if different from ship-to address)

Name ______________________

Title/Position ______________________

Company/Institution ______________________

Address ______________________
(Please supply street address for UPS shipping)

____

City ____________ State/Province ____________

Zip/Postal Code ____________ Country ____________

Tel ( ) ______________________

Fax ( ) ______________________

Email Address ______________________

Qty.	Product Code	Title	Price

Subtotal ________

MD Residents add 5% Sales Tax ________

Shipping and Handling (see box below) ________

Total Payment Enclosed ________

❑ **New Edition No Obligation Standing Order Program**
Please enroll me in this program for the products I have ordered. Government Institutes will notify me of new editions by sending me an invoice. I understand that there is no obligation to purchase the product. This invoice is simply my reminder that a new edition has been released.

15 DAY MONEY-BACK GUARANTEE

If you're not completely satisfied with any product, return it undamaged within 15 days for a full and immediate refund on the price of the product.

Shipping and Handling

Within U.S:
1-4 products: $6/product
5 or more: $4/product

Outside U.S:
Add $15 for each item (Global)

Sales Tax

Maryland 5%
Tennessee 6%
Texas 8.25%
Virginia 4.5%

SOURCE CODE: BP01

www.ingramcontent.com/pod-product-compliance
Ingram Content Group UK Ltd.
Pitfield, Milton Keynes, MK11 3LW, UK
UKHW051419150926
475561UK00005B/244